UK CHRISTMAS NUMBER ONES
1952-2022

FELIX MENSAH

First published in Great Britain in 2023
Copyright © Felix Mensah 2023
Published by Victor Publishing - victorpublishing.co.uk
Felix Mensah has asserted his right under the Copyright, Designs
and Patents Act 1988 to be identified as the author of this work.

All rights reserved. No part of this publication may be reproduced,
distributed, or transmitted in any form or by any means, including
photocopying, recording, or other electronic or mechanical methods, without the prior
written permission of the author.

ISBN: 9798865654575

www.victorpublishing.co.uk

INTRODUCTION

Since 1952, the UK singles chart has always been a regular fixture in popular culture, especially the one published at Christmas time just, to find out who has won that much coveted number one spot.

Every single since 1952 that has topped the UK chart at Christmas is featured here. They include the obvious Christmas-themed favourites, charity singles, quirky off-beat tracks, countless remakes, the odd re-issue, rock classics, reality contest winners and teen-targeted acts who have all held that coveted Christmas top spot.

We delve deeper into the progression of sales patterns, generic and artistic trends as well as the change of recorded music formats and the way we purchase them. We also take a look at how it all started. With ten inch shellac resin discs quickly followed by the newer formats eligible for chart compilers. These include the more accessible and familiar seven inch and latterly twelve inch vinyl, cassette singles, and multi-tracked CD singles through to the modern day purchase technology of digital downloads from computers and laptops.

The rundown to the Christmas number one single is always an event, if only to see what the British record buying public have chosen to dominate the festive season. From the tame traditional MOR balladry of Al Martino's *Here In My Heart* way back in 1952, to the madcap but well-intentioned LadBaby in 2022, this is the ultimate guide to those number one singles.

To achieve the tremendous task of putting this project together I had to sit down and sift through numerous magazine & paper clippings, reference books and websites to see this project throughout the planning stages. I hope I have achieved it's intended goal and that was to make it both topical and enjoyable.

If it wasn't for the following publications and sites this project would never have came to be: Joel Whitburn/Record Research/Billboard publications Top R&B Singles 1942-1999, Billboard Book Of Top 40 Hits, Top Adult Contemporary 1961-1993 & Top Country Singles 1944-1997, Billboard Book Of Number One Albums by Craig Rosen & published by Billboard, Billboard Book of Number One Hits by Fred Bronson & published by Billboard, The Guinness Book Of

UK CHRISTMAS NUMBER ONES 1952-2022

British Hit Singles & Albums, The Virgin Book of British Hit Singles - Complete UK Chart Data from 1952-2010, The Sound Of Philadelphia by Tony Cummings & published by Metheun, Baby That Is Rock & Roll by Spencer Leigh & John Firminger & published by Finbarr International, Halfway To Paradise by Spencer Leigh & John Firminger & published by Finbarr International, NME, Blacksheep Magazine, Record Mirror, Smash Hits Magazine, Blues & Soul, Echoes,Q, All Music Guide, Record Collector, Wikipedia, Encyclopedia Of Popular Music, The Official UK Charts Company & Everyhit.com.

I'd personally like to thank the following people who inspired and influenced me to pursue this project and made the hard work and research all the more worthwhile but more importantly very special:

Sharon Davis, Dave Randle, Dave McAleer, Ralph Tee, Brian J Webster of Rutland Records, Rachael Ryan, all those that I encountered at Radio Nene Valley (too numerous to mention), Bobby Eli, Lindsay Wesker, Duncan Payne, Eugene Williams Jr, Willie Morgan, Paul Gray of MKFM, James Murphy, Mark Harrington of the 'Motown Café' celebration group, Craig Sullivan, Rumour Castro, Shaun EB, Steven Edlin, Emma-Claire Young, Aden Southall, 'Lloyd' Bevan, 'Funkenstein' Marsh, Matt Facer of Soulvit , Joel Whitburn, David Nathan, Paddy Grady of PGI Ents, Frank Elson, Mark Devlin, Juls Doherty, D.A aka Deren Ali, Lev-G, Lacey, E-Money, Eric Izzle, Justin III Sublyminal English, Valley Joe, Ralph Burg, Jay Quinn, Sheraz Yousaf, David 'DRV' Veale, Adam 'Venom Adda' Williams, Aaron Poole, John Portelli aka DJ John John, Steven 'Car Wash' Altman, 'Beamy' Jeffries, Haytham Kamal, Timmy of Booom TV, Martin, Karl, Gaz & Co of BTTOS nights, Ash Ben, David Smallwood, Steve Brookstein, Kenny Thomas, Vix Perks, Adam Jang/Yeti, SoulMo Funk, Tony 'Soul Explosion Hull' Stephenson, Joelle Valente, all those at Yum Yums & Buzz Nites, Riq & Jeremy of RAGE Entertainment, Maison Quatro, Stuart Wilkie and 'Bob' & Vijay of M2F.

Thanks also to Richard Price for the option choice offer of visual use.

Big thanks to Paul Preece - officially my longest surviving school friend.

Big thanks also to all those other artists, DJs and record buyers that made this project from a possibility into a serious reality.

Also remembering those music loving friends cruelly taken away so soon:

Criss Brand, with your love of music you would've been proud of this book as would Richard I Parker and Michael 'Recycled Teenager' Smith. It is a shame you never got to see this finished product as you hoped to.

Not forgetting Jaxx MacKenzie. You are probably going to read this book from page to page in that Spanish sunshine. Steve Mullen - I hope the musical education to seek out those 'outside the box' genres inspired you to do just that. And all you other 'cats' that I have not mentioned in name (you know who you are!) and family who are still making sure that everything is kept real and grounded. Radio Nene Valley for that first positive knock on the door and all the folks at the Northamptonshire County Council Central Library for stopping me becoming part of your furniture!

Special thanks (again!) to the legendary Sharon Davis for initially making it palatable for readership and for planting that seed of inspiration for me to actually do this project to begin with.

And a big thank you to Merv Payne of Victor Publishing for sticking to your word to help finally get this project finally out there when there were times I didn't think it was possible.

This book is dedicated to the memories of:
PKA Mensah (1931-2017)
and EM Mensah (1939-2022)

Fe' Mensah 2023

UK CHRISTMAS NUMBER ONES 1952-2022

ABOUT THE AUTHOR

Fe' Mensah was born in south London but raised in the East Midlands. He occasionally contributes to the online R&B magazine '*Blacksheep*' and in the past was a regular contributor to the alternative DIY arts fanzine '*Fatdog*'. Writing assignments and music is his passionate hobby, combined the Christmas UK Number One Singles being his first full-on project - with hopefully more in years to come.

UK CHRISTMAS NUMBER ONES 1952-2022

UK CHRISTMAS NUMBER ONES 1952-2022

CONTENTS

1952 HERE IN MY HEART - AL MARTINO xx
1953 ANSWER ME - FRANKIE LAINE xx
1954 LET'S HAVE A PARTY - WINIFRED ATWELL xx
1955 CHRISTMAS ALPHABET - DICKIE VALENTINE xx
1956 JUST WALKIN IN THE RAIN - JOHNNIE RAY xx
1957 MARY'S BOY CHILD - HARRY BELAFONTE xx
1958 IT'S ONLY MAKE BELIEVE - CONWAY TWITTY xx
1959 WHAT DO YOU WANNA MAKE THOSE EYES AT ME FOR?
      - EMILE FORD & THE CHECKMATES xx
1960 I LOVE YOU - CLIFF RICHARD & THE SHADOWS xx
1961 MOON RIVER - DANNY WILLIAMS xx
1962 RETURN TO SENDER - ELVIS PRESLEY xx
1963 I WANT TO HOLD YOUR HAND - THE BEATLES xx
1964 I FEEL FINE - THE BEATLES xx
1965 DAY TRIPPER/WE CAN WORK IT OUT - THE BEATLES xx
1966 THE GREEN GREEN GRASS OF HOME - TOM JONES xx
1967 HELLO GOODBYE - THE BEATLES xx
1968 LILY THE PINK - THE SCAFFOLD xx
1969 TWO LITTLE BOYS - ROLF HARRIS xx
1970 I HEAR YOU KNOCKING - DAVE EDMUNDS xx
1971 ERNIE - BENNY HILL xx
1972 LONG HAIRED LOVER FROM LIVERPOOL - LITTLE JIMMY OSMOND .. xx
1973 MERRY XMAS EVERYBODY - SLADE xx
1974 LONELY THIS CHRISTMAS - MUD xx
1975 BOHEMIAN RHAPSODY - QUEEN xx
1976 WHEN A CHILD IS BORN (SOLEADO) - JOHNNY MATHIS xx
1977 MULL OF KINTYRE/GIRLS SCHOOL - WINGS xx
1978 MARY'S BOY CHILD/OH MY LORD - BONEY M xx
1979 ANOTHER BRICK IN THE WALL (PART II) - PINK FLOYD xx
1980 THERE'S NO ONE QUITE LIKE GRANDMA
      - ST WINIFRED'S SCHOOL CHOIR xx

UK CHRISTMAS NUMBER ONES 1952-2022

1981	DON'T YOU WANT ME - HUMAN LEAGUE	xx
1982	SAVE YOUR LOVE - RENEE & RENATO	xx
1983	ONLY YOU - FLYING PICKETS	xx
1984	DO THEY KNOW IT'S CHRISTMAS? - BAND AID	xx
1985	MERRY CHRISTMAS EVERYONE - SHAKIN' STEVENS	xx
1986	REET PETITE - JACKIE WILSON	xx
1987	ALWAYS ON MY MIND - PET SHOP BOYS	xx
1988	MISTLETOE & WINE - CLIFF RICHARD	xx
1989	DO THEY KNOW IT'S CHRISTMAS? - BAND AID II	xx
1990	SAVIOUR'S DAY - CLIFF RICHARD	xx
1991	BOHEMIAN RHAPSODY - QUEEN	xx
1992	I WILL ALWAYS LOVE YOU - WHITNEY HOUSTON	xx
1993	MR BLOBBY - MR BLOBBY	xx
1994	STAY ANOTHER DAY - EAST 17	xx
1995	EARTH SONG - MICHAEL JACKSON	xx
1996	2 BECOME 1 - SPICE GIRLS	xx
1997	TOO MUCH - SPICE GIRLS	xx
1998	GOODBYE - SPICE GIRLS	xx
1999	I HAVE A DREAM - WESTLIFE	xx
2000	CAN WE FIX IT? - BOB THE BUILDER	xx
2001	SOMETHIN' STUPID - ROBBIE WILLIAMS & NICOLE KIDMAN	xx
2002	SOUND OF THE UNDERGROUND - GIRLS ALOUD	xx
2003	MAD WORLD - MICHAEL ANDREWS FT GARY JULES	xx
2004	DO THEY KNOW IT'S CHRISTMAS? - BAND AID 20	xx
2005	THAT'S MY GOAL - SHAYNE WARD	xx
2006	A MOMENT LIKE THIS - LEONA LEWIS	xx
2007	WHEN YOU BELIEVE - LEON JACKSON	xx
2008	HALLELUJAH - ALEXANDRA BURKE	xx
2009	KILLING IN THE NAME - RAGE AGAINST THE MACHINE	xx
2010	WHEN WE COLLIDE - MATT CARDLE	xx
2011	WHEREVER YOU ARE - MILITARY WIVES CHOIR	xx
2012	HE AIN'T HEAVY, HE'S MY BROTHER - THE JUSTICE COLLECTIVE	xx
2013	SKYSCRAPER - SAM BAILEY	xx
2014	SOMETHING I NEED - BEN HAENOW	xx
2015	A BRIDGE OVER YOU - THE LEWISHAM AND GREENWICH NHS CHOIR	xx
2016	'ROCKABYE' - CLEAN BANDIT FT SEAN PAUL & ANNE-MARIE	xx
2017	PERFECT - ED SHEERAN	xx
2018	WE BUILT THIS CITY - LADBABY	xx
2019	I LOVE SAUSAGE ROLLS - LADBABY	xx
2020	DON'T STOP ME EATIN' - LADBABY	xx
2021	SAUSAGE ROLLS FOR EVERYONE - LADBABY	xx
2022	FOOD AID - LADBABY	xx

UK CHRISTMAS NUMBER ONES 1952-2022

1952

HERE IN MY HEART/
I CRIED MYSELF TO SLEEP
AL MARTINO

In 1952 the British Singles Chart was officially recognised by the respected music weekly New Musical Express, but the first official number one single at Christmas was not provided by a domestic act, but rather an Italian-American middle-of-the-road singer. Al Martino was his name, with the song "Here In My Heart".

Born Alfred Cini in Philadelphia, USA, in 1927, Al Martino worked as a bricklayer. He also sang in local clubs until he took the advice of his friend and mentor, the opera singer Mario Lanza who suggested a relocation to New York. Once there, Martino won the CBS TV show Arthur Godfrey's Talent Scouts and was quickly signed to the small BBS label for which the emotive "'Here In My Heart" was recorded. Written by Bill Borelli, Pat Genaro and Lou Levison, the song has a considerable vocal range and instrumental arrangement - and, incidentally, intended originally for Mario Lanza, was distributed nationally by Capitol Records. The company eventually acquired the rights to the master and artist, with the result that the single topped the UK chart for nine weeks, including the Christmas week of 1952. It spent eighteen weeks on the chart altogether.

His successful breakthrough came at a price - $75,000. Allegedly this was the financial protection demanded by the Mafia when they took over control of his management contract. Due to this he relocated to the UK for six years which allowed him to capitalise on his British popularity, like topping the bill at the London Palladium, while watching his decline in his homeland. Martino's British chart success was initially consistent, as he scored further major hits over the next three years including "Now", "Wanted" and "The Story of Tina" which reached the top ten. However, versions of "Summertime" and "Love You Because", issued in 1960 and 1963 respectively, were chart strugglers. Happily, all was not lost in America because he found his natural niche on the Adult Contemporary singles chart scoring consecutive hits right into the 1970s. Not only did he score on this listing but also crossed over on the R&B, Country, and Dance charts - a decade before Scottish songstress Sheena Easton enjoyed the same achievement.

The photogenic and talented Al Martino later moved into acting, and when he took the role of Sinatra-esque singer Johnny Fontane in The Godfather series of films, he not only acted but recorded the titles "Speak, Sofly Love" and "I

Have But One Heart" for the first film in 1972. As his vocal style was similar to Frank Sinatra, Dean Martin and/or Perry Como, Martino went on to enjoy considerable success on the cabaret circuit.

"Here In My Heart" is one song that refused to fade away! It was re-issued in 1961 but failed to enjoy the same success as its original 1952 outing. However the re-issued love song "Spanish Eyes" gave Martino a surprise British top five hit during the summer of 1973, while in 1978 the ironically titled "One Last Time" flopped in the UK. And it lived up to its name when it also struggled in the US Hot 100. In 1982 his contract with Capitol Records expired.

Into the new millennium, Al Martino continued to perform, and planned to write his autobiography. He recorded a new album titled "Style", and later played an ageing singer in the short film Cutout. Active into advancing age, it was a shock to hear that on 13 October 2009, six days after his 82nd birthday, the singer peacefully passed away in his Springfield, Philadelphia home.

Of his many legacies, one was (of course) to be known as the artist who recorded the first ever registered British number one single - and the first ever Christmas number one single.

A musical landmark indeed.

UK CHRISTMAS NUMBER ONES 1952-2022

1953

ANSWER ME/ BLOWING WILD
FRANKIE LAINE

This year's number one was tainted with the bizarre. Laine's single replaced Yorkshireman David Whitfield's version of the same song from the top of the chart. Both were banned by the BBC following complaints from listeners that the song mocked religion by mentioning the Lord's name, but this only made the demand greater. In this case, Laine's version sat at the top for eight weeks.

According to Wikipedia, four weeks later *both* versions sat in the pole position. Later, Whitfield and Laine re-recorded the song, amended the lyrics, and changed the title to "Answer Me, My Love". Remember: this was the pre-rock 'n' roll era!

Italian-American vocalist Frankie Laine was born Frank Paul LoVecchio, to Sicilian immigrants in Chicago's Little Italy, Illinois, in 1913. His barber father had once cut Al Capone's hair, while his grandfather was a victim of a mob killing. Laine worked as a dance teacher, singing waiter and a spa singer, and it was the latter that got him discovered by Hoagy Carmichael. With a vocal style similar to Paul Robeson, Frankie's first gold disc was for the 1947 hit "That's My Desire". Released by Mercury Records, the single charted higher on the R&B listing than on the mainstream chart, because black record buyers and radio programmers assumed the singer was African-American.

Three years later he married actress Nanette Gray, made his acting debut in the film When You're Smiling, and with his producer Mitch Miller, switched labels from Mercury to CBS/Columbia. Then in 1953, Frankie Laine scored his best performance as a top selling singles artist by dominating the chart for 18 weeks with a powerful reading of "I Believe", before closing the year with the equally dramatic "Answer Me". The origins behind this Gerhard Winkler and Fred Rauch composition lay in Germany where it was known as 'Mutterlein'. The lyrics were translated into English by Carl Sigman.

Under the guidance of Mitch Miller, the singer continued to be successfully consistent on the UK chart into the early 1960s.

"Answer Me" enjoyed a life of its own because as well as the aforementioned two versions, it returned to the UK Top 10 in 1976 courtesy of Scottish singer Barbara Dickson.

Like many acts of the 1950s, Frankie Laine concentrated on touring the middle-of-the-road circuit when the hits dried up, and by the mid 1980s he had retired to San Diego, California. In 1996 he was awarded a Lifetime Achievement Award by the Songwriters Hall Of Fame despite not being widely accepted as a composer of note.

In February 2007 at the grand age of 93 years, Frankie Laine died at home. The charts had said its final farewell to its first big voiced superstar.

1954

LET'S HAVE ANOTHER PARTY (PART 1)/ LET'S HAVE ANOTHER PARTY (PART 2)
WINIFRED ATWELL

Winifred Atwell was a 'first' when it comes to the British singles chart. Not only was she the first female instrumentalist and first black act to top the chart, but also the first black instrumentalist to hit the UK Christmas number one position. To date she still holds that record.

Winifred Atwell was born in 1915 in Tunapuna, Trinidad, where she trained as a pharmacist to work in her family's business. She mastered the piano and as a youngster played at the US Air Force base, entertaining the servicemen. Early in the 1940s, she moved to America, where she studied with Alexander Borovsky, before moving to London in 1946 to study at The Royal Academy of Music. She planned to become a concert pianist. However, this was put on hold when she married Lew Lewisohn, a variety hall agent, who persuaded her to replace her classical ambitions for a singalong 'knees-up' or 'boogie woogie' style – which would later become her much loved trademark. The 1950s was, on the whole, a chart haven for instrumentalists, because as well as Atwell, trumpeter Eddie Calvert, guitarist Bert Weedon, and fellow pianists Joe Henderson and Russ Conway were also charting names. As her popularity quickly grew, her hands were (reportedly) insured for £40,000. And it was her 'honky-tonk' playing style that formed the basis for her Christmas UK chart-topper, her 6th single.

Released by Philips Records, 'Let's Have A Party' was a medley of singalong, party favourites - "Lily Of Languna", "Honeysuckle And The Bee", "The Bear", "Nellie Dean", "Another Little Drink Wouldn't Do Us Any Harm", "Broken Doll", "Somebody Stole My Girl", "The Sheik Of Araby", "Bye Bye Blackbird", "I Wonder Where My Baby Is Tonight" and "When The Red Red Robin (Comes Bob Bob Bobbin' Along)". No-one could resist joining in, and it was this, her mixture of classical and ragtime, with an underlying invitation to enjoy an impromptu party, that was the winning formula for her chart career - ensuring she was one of the most consistent singles act during the 1950s.

When her style was deemed 'old fashioned', she returned to Trinidad, but later settled in Australia, where she was a popular artist. In 1980, she suffered a stroke, and retired a year later. Following a heart attack in 1983, Atwell died in February, and was buried alongside her husband Lew in a private cemetery, near Lismore, New South Wales.

Alongside her musical skills, Winifred Atwell turned talent scout when she discovered a London bus driver Terry Parsons. He later became balladeer Matt Monro, who went on to enjoy an incredibly successful career during the 1960s, taking his stage surname from Atwell's father.

With music ever-changing it seems more unlikely than likely that another female instrumentalist will top the UK singles chart. So, for the time being, Winifred Atwell is indeed a pioneer - and a one-off!

UK CHRISTMAS NUMBER ONES 1952-2022

1955

CHRISTMAS ALPHABET/ WHERE ARE YOU TONIGHT?
DICKIE VALENTINE

This song was written by Buddy Kaye and Jules Loman, and first recorded by Italian-American superstar crooner Perry Como under the title "A-You're Adorable". In 1954, US singing trio, The McGuire Sisters had already recorded a version of Valentine's Christmas chart topper as the B-side of "Give Me Your Heart For Christmas".

Perry Como's original incorporated each letter from the alphabet as compliments for his girlfriend – "A: You're adorable, B: You're so beautiful..." and so on. The re-write, on the other hand, repeated the idea but featured Christmas: "C: – is for the candy trimmed around the Christmas tree, H: is for the happiness with all the family". Its twee-ness was infectious fun, perfect for the festive season, but more importantly established Dickie Valentine as a top entertainer. He was also the first artist to top the UK singles chart at the start of a year (1955) with "Finger Of Suspicion" and close the year with a Christmas chart topper.

Born Richard Maxwell in November 1929 in Marylebone, London, his first acting role was as a three-year-old in the film Jack's The Boy. In between times, he trained as a singer, and while working as a call boy at Her Majesty's Theatre in London, he was overheard practising by actor Bill O'Connor who paid for him to be professionally trained as a singer. As a late teenager, Valentine was seen by music publisher Sid Green, performing in the Panama Club. Green introduced him to band leader Ted Heath, who conducted the most successful British orchestra of the time. Heath hired him to work alongside Denis Lotis and Lita Roza. This led to him working with producer Dick Rowe, who signed him to Decca Records.

Dickie Valentine was Britain's pop prince of the 1950s. He was invited to appear on The Royal Command Performance, and later headlined at The London Palladium, where he not only sang but impersonated his equals like Mario Lanza and Johnny Ray. He was truly at the top of his profession as an entertainer until mid to late 1950s, which led to his own television series Calling Dickie Valentine. In 1966, ATV gave him his own self-titled show, where he was paired with Peter Sellers to great success.

He was also a chart regular until 1959 with top selling titles like his first chart-topper "Broken Wings", "All The Time And Everywhere", "I Wonder", "Old Piano

Rag" and a couple of Festive singles ("Christmas Island" and "Snowbound For Christmas"). But the fickle record buying market turned its attention elsewhere, leading to the singer's decline. Even a switch of record labels from Decca to Pye, and then to Philips, didn't remedy the situation. American and further UK chart success eluded him, but he continued to be a popular live draw, until his early death. While travelling to an engagement at The Double Diamond Club in Caerphilly, Wales, Dickie Valentine and his musician friends Sid Boatman and Dave Pearson died in a car accident. Valentine was driving his wife's car, with which he was unfamiliar, and lost control on a dangerous part of the road, which he'd driven down many times. It was 4.20am, on 6 May 1971, and the coroner's verdict was 'death by misadventure'. Dickie Valentine was 41 years old. He is interned at Slough Crematorium.

An artist who was considered to be a cross-decade cultural casualty of 'out with the old, in with the new', Dickie Valentine's chart success might have been confined to a decade, but with 14 hits, spanning a total of six years and 92 weeks on the chart, he didn't do too badly did he?

1956

JUST WALKIN' IN THE RAIN/ IN THE CANDLELIGHT
JOHNNIE RAY

**Emotional pop ballad singer Johnnie Ray was born in Dallas, Oregon, in January 1927. He was partially deafened at the age of nine following a trampoline accident while a boy scout, and wore a hearing aid from fourteen years old. (He had surgery in 1958 which left him deaf in both ears) He was raised on a farm where he lived with his parents in Polk County, before moving to Portland, where he was educated.
As a youngster he loved music and sought inspiration from Kay Starr, Ivory Joe Hunter, among others, to develop a style that crossed pop and R&B.**

It was R&B/blues singer LaVern Baker and her manager Al Green who encouraged a young Johnnie to pursue singing as a career and to this end helped him win a record contract with the CBS/Columbia Records' subsidiary Okeh in 1951. That same year, CBS producer and A&R man Mitch Miller produced two singles, "The Little White Cloud That Cried" and "Cry", on which the vocal group The Four Lads provided the back up vocals and which were issued as a double-A sided single to top the US chart in 1951. It sold two million copies and elevated him into the teen idol league, which in turn led to him starring alongside Ethel Merman in the film "There's No Business Like Show Business", from which his single "If You Believe" was lifted. As a singer, Ray had by now developed his own on-stage style that included crying and pulling at his hair. His audiences were mesmerised by his performances. During 1952, Ray married Marilyn Morrison, despite him being arrested twice for soliciting men for sex. For the first he pleaded guilty and was fined; the second time he was found not guilty. His marriage ended in divorce in 1954.

Before dominating the 1956 Christmas UK singles chart, the singer charted with a staggering 14 consecutive UK top twenty hits including "Walking My Baby Back Home" (his first); "Faith Can Move Mountains"; two duets with Doris Day – "Ma Says Pa Says" and "Lets Walk That-a-Way"; his first UK chart topper "Such A Night"; "Who's Sorry Now" and "Ain't Misbehavin'".

Despite its feel-good nature, "Just Walkin' In The Rain" has a tale of tragedy behind it. Johnny Bragg and Robert Riley, two inmates of the Tennessee State Prison, wrote it while on laundry duty three years prior to it being recorded. Riley wrote down the lyrics spoken by Bragg, who was illiterate, with the promise of him being credited as a co-writer. A Tennessee native, Johnny

Bragg was sentenced to nearly one hundred years in prison after an alleged fit-up by state police for multiple rapes during his teens. While incarcerated, Bragg was subjected to vicious beatings, but a new governor, Frank Clement, was so sympathetic to his brutal lifestyle that he encouraged him to pursue his music by forming an group with fellow like minded convicts.

Naming themselves The Prisonaires, the R&B quintet was signed by producer Sam Philips to a Sun Records contract where "Just Walkin' In The Rain" was first recorded. The song came to the attention of Mitch Miller who believed it could cross over into the Pop market. He, in turn, persuaded Johnnie Ray to record it, believing it could be a runaway hit for him. His instincts were proved right. The song spent 23 weeks in the US top forty; peaking at number two. When released as a single in the UK, it spent seven weeks atop the chart in late 1956. British audiences were certainly warming to the 'crying man'.

After the song's success, things looked up for Johnny Bragg, who was now in his early thirties, and a free man. He embarked upon a solo musical career which included performing at the Grand Ole Opry (usually reserved for country music acts). He supported Sammy Davis Jnr at Las Vegas, and released poor-selling, up tempo soul single titled "They're Talking About Me".

Meanwhile, Johnnie Ray - after topping the UK chart in summer 1957 with "Yes Tonight Josephine" - saw his chart career decline over the next two years. As the 1960s dawned, his emotive 'crying' style was considered outdated, particularly with the growing popularity of tougher R&B, and rock 'n' roll sounds. Johnnie found himself relegated to cabaret circuits and extended touring schedules across North America, and throughout Europe and Australia.

The singer was an alcoholic and was diagnosed with cirrhosis of the liver during the early 1960s. This was instrumental in his death from organ failure in February 1990 at the Cedars-Sinai Hospital, Los Angeles. He is buried in the Hopewell Cemetary, Oregon. On the other hand, although Johnny Bragg spent part of his life behind bars, he died a free and respectable man in 2004.

UK CHRISTMAS NUMBER ONES 1952-2022

1957

MARY'S BOY CHILD/ VENEZUELA
HARRY BELAFONTE

In future years he was known as a dedicated activist in the Civil Rights Movement and campaigner against Third World poverty, but in 1957 Harry Belafonte was crowned Calypso King, thanks to a Jester Hairston composition that featured just the right ingredients for a Christmas hit. A fact proven twice over when the single was re-released for the next two festive seasons.

African-Caribbean Harry Belafonte was born in March 1927 in the Lying-In Hospital, Harlem, New York. From 1932 for eight years he moved to Jamaica to live with his grandmother. He returned to attend school, before joining the Navy to fight during the Second World War. Once discharged, he worked as a caretaker, where a resident gave him tickets for the American Negro Theatre. He was hooked! During this time, he befriended (future actor) Sidney Poitier and together they became regular theatre goers when finances permitted. Although Harry's first love was folk music, it was to acting that he first turned. To pay for lessons at the Drama Workshop, he sang in New York nightclubs, where he became a popular entertainer. After unsuccessfully launching his recording career in 1949 on the Roost label, he joined RCA Records during the early 1950s, where he ditched his folk music ambitions to record calypso, the music that reflected his roots. Belafonte soon scored global hits with "The Banana Boat Song", "Mama Look At Bubu" and "Jamaica Farewell," but a seven week stay at the top of the UK chart in late 1957 provided him with his biggest hit here.

In 1948 he married Marguerite Byrd. They divorced in 1957, whereupon he wed Julia Robinson. Then in 2008, he married for the third time, to Pamela Frank.

Harry Belafonte perhaps came across as a 'one trick pony' because his commercialised brand of calypso music and his major chart success was limited to the 1950s and early 1960s. While he was a successful singer, his recording contract with RCA expired in 1970, so he took to touring the world. It was a recording career that earned him six gold discs, and Grammys for the "Swing Dat Hammer" and "An Evening With Belafonte/Makeba" in 1960 and 1965 respectively. He also guested on peak-time television shows like The Muppet Show in 1978, on which he performed "Day-O" – a TV first! He also sang "Turn The World Around" with the Muppets wearing African tribal masks. Instead of diversifying musically, he concentrated on an acting career. His debut role was co-starring with Dorothy Dandridge in the 1953 movie Bright Road, followed a year later by Carmen Jones. He went on to star in films like the 1959 Odds Against Tomorrow, and in the early 1970s when he paired up with his friend and fellow civil rights activist, Sidney Poitier in the comedies The Buck & The Preacher and Uptown Saturday Night.

In 1959 he hosted a nationwide US special Tonight With Belafonte, from which his duet with Odetta titled "There's A Hole In My Bucket" became a US and UK hit during 1961. He won an Emmy award for the show. The same year, at Frank Sinatra's request, Belafonte performed with others at John F Kennedy's inaugural gala. In 1968, when he appeared as a guest on a Petula Clark US television special, there was public outcry because the two artists made physical contact. This upset Chrysler-Plymouth, the show's sponsors, who demanded the 'touch' sequences be removed for fear of enraging conservative America. The demands fell on silent ears, and the television special was screened in all its glory.

Harry Belafonte's career as an entertainer is well documented and his name also gives him instant recognition as a humanitarian and civil rights activist. Little did he realise that when he introduced calypso into mainstream pop with his version of "Mary's Boy Child" he gave the UK its first calypso-infused chart topper. The single also returned to the top spot 21 years later courtesy of 1970's group Boney M (see 1978).

Since those days, Harry later became a UNICEF goodwill ambassador, and as such he helped raise funds for the plight of Rwandan children, and in, 2001 supported the HIV-AIDS campaign in South Africa. Four years later visited Kenya to instigate an educational programme to beat the disease. In 2006 Belafonte received the BET Humanitarian Award, one of several honours bestowed upon him for his tireless humanitarian work. Perhaps the most publicised fund raising activity was as one of the organisers of the USA For Africa charity extravaganza, which was the American version of Band Aid (see 1984). His involvement resulted in a renewed interest in his music, leading to a recording deal with EMI Records. "Paradise In Gazankulu", released during 1988, featured protest songs against Aparthied.

An active campaigner, that was never far away from the public eye, Harry Belafonte sadly passed away from congestive heart failure at his home in Manhattan, New York City on April 25, 2023, at the age of 96.

The definition of a full-life lived.

UK CHRISTMAS NUMBER ONES 1952-2022

1958

IT'S ONLY MAKE BELIEVE/ I'LL TRY
CONWAY TWITTY

A rock 'n' roll ballad, performed and co-written by an American with a unusual stage name, was this year's Christmas number one single. It was also his first UK hit.

Conway Twitty was born Harold Lloyd Jenkins, in September 1933 in Friars Point, Mississippi. His family moved to Helena, Arkansas, while he was still a youngster, and it was there he headed up the Phillips County Ramblers vocal group. This later led to him hosting his own Saturday morning radio show. When Conway was drafted into the US Army, he was stationed in the Far East, where he formed another group, The Cimmerons. Upon his discharge, he starting writing his own material and recorded under his birth name, under the aegis of Sun Records producer Sam Philips. Nothing was released, leaving him free to try elsewhere. However, he first needed to change his name.

Inspired by road signs which he spotted on his travels - Conway (in Arkansas), Twitty (in Texas), he decided to adopt them for the quirky stage name. After an unsuccessful stint at Mercury Records where he attracted a reasonable following in Canada, Conway Twitty joined the MGM Records roster of artists, where, the story goes, in just twenty minutes he wrote the much covered standard "It's Only Make Believe", with his drummer, Jack Nance. The song attracted controversy when they were accused of plagiarism by the writers of the French tune "(All Of A Sudden) My Heart Sings". The action was settled out of court.

'It's Only Make Believe' topped the Transatlantic singles chart for a total of seven weeks, but the British public refused to let it fade so quickly. It re-entered the chart twice during the 1970s - first, for country/pop crooner Glen Campbell in 1970, and eight years later for the boy band, Child. Conway Twitty was a consistent international chart name into the early 1960s with titles like "Story Of My Love", "Mona Lisa", "Is A Blue Bird Blue" and "C 'Est Si Bon". But when the musical landscape began changing, he sensed what was to come. Like most white singers from the Deep South, who enjoyed success in the mainstream market, he moved to Nashville to successfully switch to a country music format. In 1970, he issued "Hello Darlin'" which stayed in the C&W pole position for four weeks. His duet with Loretta Lynn "After The Fire Is Gone" was next, and as a duo, they went on to win four

Country Music Association awards. He could do no wrong as the hits followed one after the other – "Louisiana Woman, Mississippi Man"; "As Soon As I Hang Up The Phone!", "Can't Love You Enough", among others. In 1973, "You've Never Been This Far Before" was an instant US chart topper thanks to being banned by some radio DJs due to its risqué lyrics. By 1978, with the release of "The Greatest Lady Of Them All", his career was at a crossroads, but with a change of image, he issued his 50th single "Don't Call Him A Cowboy" in 1985, another number one title. Conway followed this with another five by 1990. He went on to enjoy about 100 country chart singles, 40 of which reached number one, earning him the title of the most successful singles act on the US Country Chart during the 1970s.

In the early 1980s, he opened his own tourist attraction called Twitty City in Hendersonville, Tennessee, which cost over $3 million to build. It remained poplar for over a decade, and was the subject of the BBC TV programme Entertainment USA hosted by Jonathan King.

During the 1960s Twitty also appeared in the films College Confidential, Sex Kittens Go To College, and Platinum High School.

One of his last noted recordings was on the 1994, MCA Records release "Rhythm, Country And Blues" compilation, where soul/R&B artists were paired up with country acts. Twitty duetted with Sam Moore (from the soul duo Sam & Dave) on a version of Tony Joe White's "Rainy Night In Georgia". The album hit the Country Chart at the top.

Conway Twitty died in June 1993 from an abdominal aneurysm, in the Cox South Hospital, Springfield, Missouri. He was part way through recording his last studio album "Final Touches" and just three months shy of his 60th birthday. He is best remembered for his distinctive vocal style, healthy glow and quiffed hair – and of course, a 35 year musical legacy with 110 albums and 55 number one singles.

1959

WHAT DO YOU WANT TO MAKE THOSE EYES AT ME FOR?/ DON'T TELL ME YOUR TROUBLES
EMILE FORD & THE CHECKMATES

West Indian native Emile Sweetman, was the first UK-based act to sell a million copies of a single. He was also the country's first ever black pop pin-up.

Born in October 1937 in Castries, Saint Lucia, Emile and his family moved to the UK during the mid-1950s to study at Paddington's Technical College and Tottenham's Polytechnic in London. Adopting the stage name of Emile Ford, he was unable to resist the pull of the rapidly growing British music scene. As a soloist, his first public performance was in a Kensington club, followed by others at local venues. He was twenty years old. This led to him singing with a support group, attracting television guest spots in 1958 on the music shows Oh Boy! and Six Five Special. A year later he set up his own sound system, and formed the inter-racial group The Checkmates (which included his brother George) to support him on stage. As such, they entered a talent competition, where the prize was recording sessions produced by Joe Meek, plus a contract with Pye Records. Emile Ford and the Checkmates won, and soon hit the studios to record their first single.

Pye Record's A&R suits decided their first single was to be a cover of "Don't Tell Me Your Troubles", penned by US country singer Don Gibson. The B-side was to be a version of an old music hall tune recently recorded by US band leader Johnny Otis. Titled "What Do You Want To Make Those Eyes At Me For?", it apparently took Otis a mere fifteen minutes to record in two takes. Having heard the finished product, Pye decided to promote the B-side to the topside.

This perky tune spent six weeks at the top the UK singles chart, it earned Emile his first gold disc, and although a tremendous start to his career, Emile

UK CHRISTMAS NUMBER ONES 1952-2022

Ford wasn't going to be a future chart name. In fact, his career as a singles act was relatively short lived because, perhaps, the UK wasn't ready for its own black pop pin-up. Another factor was the song itself was too strong to follow up. Thanks to its chart-topping status, Pye Records placed the track with the US independent label, Andie, in an attempt to repeat the success. The move flopped, leaving the record company to concentrate on the UK market.

Emile Ford wasn't a one hit wonder by any means, he released an EP titled 'Emile' which spent a trio of weeks at the pole positon of the short-lived EP chart and scored seven further hit singles in the early sixties including a version of the Frank Losser composition "On A Slow Boat To China" which clinched third position. A change of direction came with his next release "You'll Never Know What You're Missing", a number two hit, followed by his version of the Billie Holiday standard "Them There Eyes" which peaked at number eight. Just as it seemed he was on the decline, Emile Ford released "Counting Teardrop" which returned him to the top five. It was a short lived success because "I Wonder Who's Kissing Her Now" (credited to solo Emile Ford) was his last charting single in March 1962. He subsequently concentrated on his original career intentions of being a sound engineer and eventually started his own electrics firm which pioneered a marketable version of his sound system prototype.

Emile Ford's UK singles chart career spanned 89 weeks, spread over a three year period. He might have turned his back on the music industry but his chart topper has refused to fade: it was a hit for Shakin' Stevens twenty-eight years later.

1960

I LOVE YOU/ 'D' IN LOVE
CLIFF RICHARD & THE SHADOWS

Already into his second year as a chart name, the former Harry Rodger Webb, born on 14 October 1940 in Lucknow, India, moved to Britain with his parents, Rodger and Dorothy, and sisters, Donella and Jacqueline, in 1948.

They first lived in a room in Carlshalton, Surrey, where Harry attended the Stanley Park Road Primary School. During this time his father was unemployed, but in 1950 he was hired by Ferguson's Radio in Enfield, Middlesex, while his mother found factory work in Broxbourne. The family relocated to Waltham Cross, where Harry attended the King's Road Primary School in 1950, the same year as his youngest sister, Joan, was born. As he failed his eleven plus examination, Harry moved lto the Cheshunt Secondary Modern School, and the family moved for the third time - to Cheshunt. While at school, Harry became obsessed with amateur dramatics and rock 'n' roll, and was often caught playing truant watching touring shows by American acts. In 1957 he left school with one GCE 'O' Level in English and a skiffle group, known as The Quintones, was formed with school friends. It later disbanded when the three female members moved to secretarial college full time.

Harry's first job was working as a credit control clerk at the Atlas Lamps factory in Enfield, while out of working hours, he joined Terry Smart and others in the Dick Teague Skiffle Group. In time, he and Dick Teague left to form The Drifters, which led them to John Foster, who became their manager. The first thing he did was to change Harry's name to Cliff Richard, and in 1958, the renamed singer recorded a demo single of the Jerry Lee Lewis song "Breathless" and Lloyd Price's "Lawdy, Miss Clawdy at the HMV Records shop in Oxford Street, London. Regular appearances at the 21's Coffee Bar in Soho, led to Ian Samwell joining them as lead guitarist, and changing their name to Cliff Richard and the Drifters. In time, one of their demo recordings came to the attention of Norrie Paramor, head of A&R at EMI Records. He was sufficiently inspired by them to record further tracks at Abbey Road Studios. His debut single "Move It" soared to number two in the UK chart. It was originally intended that Cliff's version of Bobby Helms' "Schoolboy Crush" would be the A-side, but the public preferred its flipside!

UK CHRISTMAS NUMBER ONES 1952-2022

Following this single there was a group membership change – lead guitarist Hank Marvin (born Brian Rankin, in Newcastle, Tyne and Wear on 28 October 1941) rhythm guitarist Bruce Welch (born Bruce Cripps in Bognor Regis, Sussex, on 2 November 1941) Terry Smart on drums, and Ian Samwell. In time, Samwell was replaced by Jet Harris (born Terence Harris in Kingsbury, London on 6 July 1939) and Smart was replaced by Tony Meehan (born Daniel Meehan in London on 2 March 1943). They toured the UK with The Kalin Twins and The Most Brothers, and in December 1958 released his second single "High Class Baby", a top ten hit. Early the following year, with two hit singles to their credit, Cliff and his group embarked upon thief first headline tour with Wee Willie Harris and Jimmy Tarbuck as support acts. During 1960 there was a further change when The Drifters were forced to change their name to The Shadows because there was already an established American vocal group using the name.

Cliff and the Shadows made their television debut on Jack Good's innovative music show Oh Boy, where Cliff was told to drop his lip curling and sexy movements for fear of corrupting the younger viewers! Then in 1959, with his new group membership, Cliff started touring the UK regularly, and the hits followed one after another – "Livin' Lovin' Doll", "Mean Streak", and a pair of chart toppers with "Living Doll" and "Travellin' Light". Also this year, he appeared in his first film Serious Charge with Anthony Quayle and Sarah Churchill. Cliff played Curly Thompson, a young rock 'n' roll singer. "Living Doll" was lifted from the film soundtrack as a single in July 1959, to top the UK chart for five weeks, earning Cliff his first gold disc. Following the success of his acting debut, he was signed up to play 'Bongo' Herbert in Expresso Bongo, starring Laurence Harvey. Once again, Cliff played a rock 'n' roller. Laurence Harvey played his manager with Sylvia Sims as his girlfriend. Without a doubt, critics agreed, Cliff Richard was the British equivalent – or answer to – America's rising superstar, Elvis Presley.

Meanwhile, "Travellin' Light"/"Dynamite" entered the UK chart. The latter titled stalled in the top twenty, while the former hit the pole position where it stayed for five weeks. The single also hit the US top thirty which prompted Cliff and The Shadows to undertake a five week tour there early in 1960. "A Voice In The Wilderness" was issued in their absence. Taken from Expresso Bongo, it hit the top two, while the "Expresso Bongo" EP peaked in the top twenty.

"I Love You" was his fourth number one single, following 1960's "Please Don't Tease", and his first over the Christmas period. Written by Bruce Welch and produced by Norrie Paramor, "I Love You" spent two weeks at the top of the chart. The success of this achievement was tainted with tragedy. His father, who had told his son that the single was his favourite to date, was seriously ill in hospital at the time. Sadly, he never fully recovered, and at fifty-six years of age, he died.

Cliff Richard and The Shadows were to enjoy separate and joint careers throughout the sixties. Cliff continued to swop the microphone for the camera to forge a successful acting career for himself with his next, the highly acclaimed The Young Ones in 1962, where his co-stars included Melvyn

Hayes, Richard O'Sullivan and Carole Grey. And The Shadows! This time Cliff played Nicki, the leader of a youth club situated in a rundown area of London. The plan was to stop the club being demolished for redevelopment. "When The Girl In Your Arms Is The Girl In Your Heart"/"I Got A Funny Feeling" were lifted for release from the soundtrack to hit the top three, and the soundtrack album replaced Elvis Presley's Blue Hawaii film theme at the top of the album chart. The single "The Young Ones" entered the UK chart at the top, a position it held for six weeks, passing gold disc status, and was Cliff's biggest selling single to date.

Summer Holiday followed a year later. Another runaway success but, not only that, clothes shops did a roaring trade selling white string vests! Melvyn Hayes was hired again, alongside Una Stubbs, Ron Moody, David Kossoff, and The Shadows. The plot this time centred around the adventures enjoyed by a group of mechanics driving a London Transport double-decker bus through five European countries. A further trio of titles followed: "Summer Holiday" (his twentieth single) "Bachelor Boy", "The Next Time" and "Dancing Shoes" – while the actual film soundtrack album hit the top spot for a fourteen week run. In 1964, Wonderful Life, filmed in the Canary Islands and co-starring Una and Melvyn, plus Susan Hampshire and Richard O'Sullivan, was premiered in London. This time, Cliff and The Shadows were the entertainment on a luxury Mediterranean cruise until they lost their jobs. Whereupon, improbable as it seemed, the captain put them to sea on a raft which drifted to the Canary Islands where they became involved in the shooting of the daughter of a Sheik. In 1968 Cliff completed his next film Two A Penny, in which he played a young pedlar, Jamie Hopkins, who discovered Christianity through his girlfriend. His co-stars were Dora Bryan and Billy Graham, who produced the film. This was followed by a musical comedy Finder's Keepers centred around a nuclear bomb off the coast of Spain. Four other films followed but none as noteworthy as those highlighted previously - such as His Land in 1970, The Case two years later, Take Me High in 1973, and Run For Your Wife in 2012, where he played a cameo role.

Cliff Richard's rise to fame was extraordinary to say the least. His career appeared to emulate that of his idol Elvis Presley in as much as both turned from singer to actor; both recorded rock and ballads, and both had the support of strong management. With the stardom came his fans. Uncontrollable and hysterical, they were whipped to a frenzy at his sold-out concerts, and huge sales were made with merchandising bearing his name. With the close of the 1960s, he had won most of the prestigious industry awards, including silver and gold discs, and Ivor Novello honours. He was voted Best British Male Vocalist on numerous occasions, and was now as popular on the small screen as he was on the cinema circuit. As a singer he could do no wrong. The hits were countless – "On The Beach", "Constantly", "I Could Easily Fall (In Love With You)", "The Minute You're Gone", and so on.

The Cliff Richard phenomenon continued to grow through the 1960s. During the early part of the decade he topped the bill on television's prime entertainment show Sunday Night At The London Palladium before an estimated 19 million viewers, the largest audience to date. He went on to join a star-studded cast that included Adam Faith, Diana Dors and Max Bygraves on the Royal Variety Performance, staged at the Victoria Theatre, London.

UK CHRISTMAS NUMBER ONES 1952-2022

Among Cliff's musical achievements at this time, he had the honour (as it was then) of representing his country in the 1968 Eurovision Song Contest with the bouncy "Congratulations". Although he was the runner-up, the song gave him another UK chart topper. He was asked again to represent the UK, singing "Power To All Our Friends". This time he came third and the single hit the UK top five in March 1973.

The media affectionately nicknamed him 'The Peter Pan Of Pop' because he maintained his youthful looks and young outlook on life. His singles charted every year and he sustained a career that appealed both to those fans who grew up with him and their children, and so on.

Meanwhile, The Shadows went on to become the UK's most successful instrumental singles/albums act ever, although they never scored a Christmas number one title. That was left to Cliff who, despite his original reservations of releasing a festive single for fear of it underminding his strong Christian faith and diverting people from the true spirit of Christmas, he released "Little Town" in 1982 to peak at number one, which to be fair, was in line with his beliefs. However, it took another six years before 'Christmas Cliff' struck again, to hit the top spot with everyone's favourite "Mistletoe And Wine" which marked a twenty-eight year gap.

(See Christmas 1988 and Christmas 1990)

UK CHRISTMAS NUMBER ONES 1952-2022

1961

MOON RIVER/ A WEAVER OF DREAMS
DANNY WILLIAMS

"Moon River" was written by Henry Mancini and Johnny Mercer. It featured in the 'opposites attract' themed 1961 film Breakfast At Tiffany's starring Audrey Hepburn as Holly Golightly and George Peppard as Paul "Fred" Varjak. The romantic comedy was directed by Blake Edwards, probably best remembered for his Pink Panther film series – and marrying Julie Andrews! Influenced by Nat King Cole, Danny Williams was the song publisher's choice to record the track which went on to win Mancini the 1962 Grammy Award for Record of the Year, and Mercer, a Grammy for Song of the Year. However, it nearly didn't happen because he misunderstood a lyric in the verse. After viewing the film he had a change of heart.

Born in the South African province of Port Elizabeth on 7 January 1942 (died 6 December 2005), Danny sang professionally from his teen years. He teamed up with the touring Golden City Dixies performing across South Africa before bringing the show to the UK during 1959. While in London, Danny met up with EMI Records' Norman Newell who, impressed with his talent, signed him as a soloist. From now on, he spent most of his time in his newly adopted country. Danny's first UK hit was "We Will Never Be This Young Again" in May 1961, and was the start of eight hits that included one chart topper which was the follow-up to his second single "The Miracle Of you" in the July.

His version of "Moon River" released in November 1961, was performed in a dreamy, ethereal, almost haunting, style, which struck the hearts of record buyers to secure the UK top spot for two weeks. This much recorded song, was also recorded by soul man Jerry Butler in late 1961, Andy Williams for his album "Moon River And Other Great Movie Themes" in 1962; Aretha Franklin, Jay and the Americans, Paul Anka, Ben E King and Bobby Darin, among others, during the 1960s. Versions continue to be recorded to this day, such is the timeless appeal of the song. Danny's first hit of 1962 "Jeanne", was followed by the top ten entrant "Wonderful World Of The Young". Also this year, he appeared in the film Play It Cool, directed by Michael Winner, and starring teen idol, Billy Fury, with Helen Shapiro and Bobby Vee, among others. Fury's "Once Upon A Dream" was the film's only hit. "Tears" was the last UK hit of the year for Danny, followed by one during 1963, namely, "My Own True Love". This year saw him tour the UK with Helen Shapiro, and The Beatles as support act. Danny Williams also scored two US hits "White On White" and

"Little Toy Balloon", but with the changing musical landscape gearing towards male rock groups and/or female soloists, Williams suddenly found himself outdated. Luckily he found regular work on the often lucrative cabaret circuit. He switched labels from EMI to Decca Records, where he enjoyed a minor hit in the late 1960s with the pacey, Motown-styled "Who's Little Girl Are You", which in future years, became a dance floor favourite on the Northern Soul club scene.

Having survived a nervous breakdown in 1968 and later bankruptcy, he decided to re-launch his career as a chart name during the seventies. With a little help from the world of television advertising, he made a belated and short-lived UK chart comeback in 1977 with "Dancing Easy" released by Ensign Records. It was an adaptation of (the drink) Martini's "anytime, anyplace, anywhere" slogan, which attracted the public's imagination. So much so, the single was a top thirty hit. The follow up, a remake of Razzy's "I Hate Hate", became a significant disco hit. Then, Danny found himself back with EMI Records in the mid-1980s, when he attempted another comeback with the critically acclaimed radio hit "Green Eyes".

In later years, Danny, who was often compared to Johnny Mathis, successfully made a name for himself in the world of martial arts. While in the music world, he did what other artists of his ilk did and joined the 'oldies' tour circuit. For a decade he performed his own material and that of his early influence, Nat King Cole.

In December 2005, the man who recorded the definitive version of "Moon River" died from lung cancer. He was 63 years old.

To this day, Danny Williams' interpretation of "Moon River" remains the most popular version.

… UK CHRISTMAS NUMBER ONES 1952-2022

1962

RETURN TO SENDER/ WHERE DO YOU COME FROM
ELVIS PRESLEY

One of music's most influential artists achieved his lone Christmas chart topping single in 1962 with a song featured in the film "Girls! Girls! Girls!", in which he also starred. This was one of countless number one singles from a singer who rocked the world, yet never once stepped foot in the UK. Fans were reliant on his music and his films. But it was enough to secure him the place of music icon through the decades.

Elvis Aaron Presley born on 8th January 1935 (died 16 August 1977) in East Tupelo, Mississipi, USA, to Gladys and Vernon Presley, was the survivor of a twin sibling. They lived in a rundown neighbourhood where being members of the First Assembly Of God church helped them to survive. While at the Lawhon Grammar School, the ten-year-old Elvis Presley was encouraged to enter the "Mississippi-Alabama Fair and Dairy Show", an annual music festival. He was runner-up, singing "Old Shep", a song telling of a special relationship between a boy and his dog. In 1948, the Presley family moved to Memphis, and while his father worked at the United Paint Company and his mother became a nurse's aide, Elvis contributed to the household finances by working as a gardener. His wages enabled him to purchase his first guitar, enabling him to emulate the country and western and R&B music that he loved so much.

When he left school with no academic qualifications, Elvis worked for the Crown Electric Company as a truck driver, and whenever possible he would visit the Memphis Recording Company where it cost $4 to record a song. Sam Phillips owned the company and its subsidiary company Sun Records, and would often see Presley using the facilities but took little notice of him. However, his office manager did, and secured a tape of Elvis singing "My Happiness" and "That's When Your Heartaches Begin" to play to Phillips. These songs interested sufficiently to record him with a handful of musicians. The result was "That's All Right, Mama", and with "Blue Moon Of Kentucky" they became Presley's debut single on the Sun label. Following airtime from DJ Dewey Phillips (no relation) on his "Red, Hot And Blue" show on Memphis' premier radio station, WHBQ, Phillips received 6,000 advanced orders for the single.

In July 1954 Elvis was signed to Sun Records where his next single "Good Rockin' Tonight" was released in September, followed by "Milkcow Blues Boogie" early-1955. By now, Elvis had had a succession of managers, but it was his introduction to Colonel Tom Parker that was to change his career prospects. Parker signed a deal with Elvis and his father to take over management and promotion, handling all aspects of his future career that included recording, performing and acting, for 25% of all his earnings. But firstly, he had to wait until Elvis' management deal with Bob Neal ended. By this time, record company interest was rising. For example, Decca Records offered Sam Phillips $5,000 for Presley's contract, which was rejected. Other offers included those from Dot with $7,500, Columbia Records ($15,000) Atlantic Records ($25,000) and Mercury suggested a starting bid of $10,000. No progress was made on any of the deals.

Once Elvis Presley was contract free, one of Parker's first assignments was to secure him to a major record company deal. Following negotiations with RCA Records, a $40,000 deal was struck at the Warwick Hotel, New York City, which, when broken down, saw Elvis receive $5,000 for future royalties on past Sun Records' reissues, and $35,000 for the Sun contract. "Heartbreak Hotel" in January 1956 was Presley's debut RCA single which was his first UK chart entrant, peaking at no 2. The US release coincided with Presley's television debut on Tommy and Jimmy Dorsey's Stage Show, the first of five appearances within two months. Other television spots followed to push "Heartbreak Hotel" to the top of the US singles chart, selling over one million copies. Appearing on The Milton Berle Show to perform "I Want You, I Need You, I Love You" and "Hound Dog" prompted a huge outcry from the viewing public who swamped the television station's switchboard with complaints about Elvis' provocative hip-shaking, pelvic thrusts and vulgar leers! It was his last appearance on the show for over ten years. On further television programmes, like The Ed Sullivan Show, Elvis was filmed from the waist up. While the single topped the US chart, it peaked in the UK top twenty, with "Hound Dog" hitting the top two. Three more singles became top thirty hits during 1956, namely "Blue Moon", "I Don't Care If The Sun Don't Shine" and "Love Me Tender" from the film of the same name (originally called "The Reno Brothers") which was Presley's debut as an actor. The single had one million advanced orders – a first for a single - and the film was the first for a contract negotiated by Colonel Tom Parker with Paramount Pictures. The deal would span seven years.

Meanwhile, Presleymania was gripping the US. His unique brand of rock 'n' roll caused total mayhem and hysteria among the young and dismay among the older generation. The frenzy was translated into several hits like those which charted in the UK: "All Shook Up" (his first UK chart topper), "Jailhouse Rock", "King Creole" and "A Fool Such As I".

From his earnings, Presley purchased a two-storey mansion, Graceland, for an estimated $102,500. Then, following the release of "Don't" in March 1958 he was drafted as a private into the Army for two years.

His call-up was postponed to enable him to finish his fourth film "King Creole". When he was shipped to Fort Hood, Texas, his family followed him as this was the first time in his life that he would have been parted from his mother, Gladys. However, such was the strain on her that she died on 14 August 1958 shortly before her son was shipped to Germany. Elvis was bored by Army life but did meet his future wife, fourteen-year-old Priscilla Ann Beaulieu. In March 1960, GI 53310761, Sergeant Elvis Presley left the Army to return to the US where he found music had drastically changed in his absence, although his stock piled songs from his films ensured he was a frequent visitor to the charts.

Huge publicity surrounded his return to the music business and, of course, his first single, the powerful ballad "It's Now Or Never" which buried his rock 'n' roll past. The single, based on the Italian song "O Sole Mio" topped the UK and US charts, selling an estimated 20 million copies globally. Presleymania had spread across the world, particularly the UK, and that wasn't about to change for some time.

By 1961 Presley had starred in six films and completed his seventh "Wild In The Country" from which "Are You Lonesome Tonight?" was lifted to hit the top of the UK chart for four weeks and for six weeks in the US pole position. "Wooden Heart" was next, taken from the film "GI Blues" which he starred in after leaving the Army - another UK chart topper. Likewise the next "Surrender" and "(Marie's The Name) His Latest Flame/Little Sister", the last releases of 1961. As "Surrender" topped the world's charts, Presley was filming "Blue Hawaii" co-starring Angela Lansbury, and had raised $50,000 from his charity performance at Pearl Harbour for the USS Arizona Memorial Fund. (The Arizona was sunk with over 1,000 men on board by Japanese aircraft in 1941). It was Presley's last concert for over seven years.

Unbeknown to the public, Presley's girlfriend Priscilla had, with her parents' consent, visited him at Graceland, eventually moving in under the guardianship of Presley's father. To steer any media interest away from her, Presley publicised his affair with actress Ann-Margret. Also during this time, Elvis was a regular medication taker, prescribed for him by a handful of doctors.

"Blue Hawaii" was his most successful film to date, grossing $30 million. Hot on its heels was "Girls! Girls! Girls!", another romantic movie, and another conveyor belt production to placate the film company's demand. Singles released during 1962 included four UK number one titles – "Rock A Hula Baby", "Can't Help Falling In Love", "Good Luck Charm", "She's Not You" and "Return To Sender" from "Girls! Girls! Girls!" This up tempo single, written by Otis Blackwell and Winfield Scott, was adapted from the film, where his co-stars included Jeremy Slate, future Star Trek actress Laurel Goodwin, and Stella (Estelle Eggleston) Stevens. Produced by Steve Scholes, "Return To Sender" had a strong musical slant towards R&B, thanks to musicians like Bobby Keys, jazz guitarist Barney Kessell, and legendary Nashville saxophonist Homer 'Boots' Randolph. And this secured additional success on the R&B chart. "Return To Sender" became one of Elvis' biggest hits, despite the fact he disliked some of the songs and plots in the actual film. He had wanted to take on a serious acting role that would stretch his ability, and not that of a penniless Hawaiian fisherman with unreachable dreams. Elvis' manager, Colonel Tom Parker, had other ideas and persuaded him to take on the film's male lead and record the soundtrack. The film was a hit. The soundtrack achieved gold status (US number three/UK number two) while "Return To Sender" not only dominated the UK singles chart for three weeks, selling 700,000 copies over the Festive period, but spent five weeks at number two in his homeland with sales reaching two million. In 1993, the US Postal Service issued a commemorative postage stamp honouring Elvis Presley. It was reputed that stamp enthusiasts posted envelopes containing the stamps to fictitious addresses in the hope that they would be returned bearing the 'return to sender' rubber stamp marking.

Elvis Presley continued to outshine and outsell his competitors. His three films a year continued to generate millions of dollars, while his record sales were staggering on an international level. "Good Luck Charm" was his 16th US number one single, a record he held until The Beatles hit America. The single also topped the UK chart for five weeks and, unlike the impending situation in America, Elvis' popularity in the UK showed no signs of declining. "Good Luck Charm" was his last UK chart topper, while in the UK his luck held for another year with "(You're The) Devil In Disguise" in July 1963. "Crying In The Chapel" would be his next in 1965. Presley was so immersed in film schedules that they dominated his career. He never promoted his singles as Colonel Parker had banned him from live performances including television spots. Fans could only see him on the big screen. Being oblivious to the music industry, Elvis was unaware of the huge impact The Beatles were making during 1964 when Beatlemania began its grip on the world. The group had already toured America with riotous scenes emulating that of Presley's early career, and as Elvis was their musical hero, a meeting was arranged in August 1965. Both sides were reportedly disappointed. But it was alleged that Presley took his feelings one step further when he apparently informed the Bureau of Narcotics and Dangerous Drugs that John Lennon and Paul McCartney's compositions were substance-induced!

Elvis and Colonel Parker celebrated their tenth anniversary in March 1965, when it was revealed Presley had sold over 100 million records with estimated earnings of $150 million globally. His films had generated a further $130,000. Yet, Presley was forced to return to live performances in the early 1970s because the bulk of his fortune had been spent. Nonetheless, Elvis remained the King, and when "Crying In The Chapel" hit the top, it cemented his record sales power, also winning him his first Grammy Award for Best Sacred Performance of 1967. As the single peaked, his latest film "Tickle Me" was released, and work had begun on the next "Paradise Hawaiian Style", followed by "Harum Scarum", "Frankie And Johnny" and "Spinout". The film conveyor belt finally ended in 1969 with "Change Of Habit". In May 1967, Elvis finally married Priscilla Beaulieu during an eight-minute ceremony at The Aladdin Hotel, Las Vegas. Lisa Marie, their daughter, was born in February 1968 (died in January 2023). Four years later her parents separated.

Following a televised American showcase in 1968, Presley was encouraged to return to the recording studio, eager to record powerful, soul songs and chose to record at the American Sound Studios in Memphis, home to some of the country's most influential black singers. He recorded a year's worth of material that included "In The Ghetto", the debut single extracted from what was known as 'The Memphis Sessions'. The single re-established Presley as a top three US artist, selling over one million copies in 1969. It was a number two UK chart hit, followed by two equally impassioned songs "Suspicious Minds" and "Kentucky Rain"; number two and number 21 respectively. In the US "Suspicious Minds" sold over two million units to top the chart, while "Kentucky Rain" peaked at number six. With the release of these singles, Elvis performed at Las Vegas' International Hotel for a four-week season, guaranteeing him $1 million. His first live show since 1961. Joining him on stage were the premier soul sisters, The Sweet Inspirations, led by Cissy Houston (mother of Whitney). It was a triumphant return and secured Elvis a five year contract. Following his second $1 million season, he was hospitalised with a colon ailment attributed to his overuse of steroids. His drug dependency was also mounting and causing concern to his entourage.

Presley's live recording of "The Wonder Of You" followed "Kentucky Rain" was a UK chart topper for six weeks in 1970, but stalled in the US top ten. During the seventies, Elvis had re-established himself as a performer, while his singles were hits of varying degrees. On stage he resembled an unflattering tailor's dummy wearing high collared, wide-belted cat suits, flared trousers and heeled boots, designed to conceal his spiralling weight, the result of unhealthy eating and drug abuse. Presleymania had returned but this time, it ended dramatically and tragically.

In 1972 Presley received a Lifetime Achievement Grammy Award, and spent the year touring America. Of the singles released this year, all hit the UK top ten, namely, "Until Its Time For You To Go", "American Trilogy", "Burning Love" and "Always On My Mind". He performed a benefit concert for composer/singer Kuiokalakani Lee, who died in 1966. "Elvis: Aloha From Hawaii" was transmitted live from the Honolulu International Centre Arena across the world raising $75,000 for Lee's Cancer Trust Fund. The bulk of 1973 was spent touring, including his Las Vegas season. His divorce from Priscilla was settled, and his health worsened. His battle against obesity and high blood pressure, together with his drug dependency to function was escalating. He also relied on pain killers for muscles sprained during his performances. It was during this time that Dr Nichopoloulos "Dr Nick" established a place in Elvis' personal entourage. In 1974 Presley collapsed on tour and was hospitalised for the third time. His music continued, including the first album to be recorded in his Graceland studio, titled "From Elvis Presley Boulevard, Memphis" in 1976. In April 1977, Presley was readmitted to the Baptist Memorial Hospital in Memphis, said to be suffering from influenza and exhaustion. He then recorded what would be his last material and in June he performed his final concert at the Market Square Arena, Indianapolis.

On 16 August 1977 paramedics rushed to Graceland, where they discovered Elvis slumped in his bathroom. He was rushed to the Baptist Memorial Hospital but was pronounced dead upon arrival. Elvis Presley was 42 years old. Cause of death was thought to be drug related, but as he had an enlarged heart, among other ailments, the diagnosis leaned towards a violent heart attack. Drug abuse was secondary. His funeral was held at Graceland on 18 August, and a reputed 80,000 people lined the route from his Memphis home to Forest Hill Cemetery where Elvis was to be buried next to his mother. After attempts to steal his body, the remains of both Presley and his mother were reburied in the Meditation Garden at Graceland. The single "Way Down" meantime topped the UK chart, and his music catalogue once again returned to the international charts.

In 1979, Elvis' father Vernon died. His body was buried next to his wife and son. Midway through 1980, "Dr Nick" was indicted on numerous counts of over-prescribing drugs to eleven patients, including Elvis. He was cleared of all charges.

A survey compiled by the Guinness Book of British Hit Singles & Albums officially declared that in May 2004, Elvis Presley's UK chart life outlived his mortal life by five years - and counting! Not bad for an artist who quickly morphed from being The King Of Western Bop, to King Of Rock 'n' Roll.

Elvis Presley was hailed as the most popular music icon of our age. His death created a huge void in the industry, his influence knew no musical bounds and his international appeal from a teenage sex symbol to a maturing overweight man never quavered. The fact that he never left America did not appear to stem his popularity among the young. He was a huge influence in American life, proving, as he did, the rags to riches story actually can work. He was the American Dream; and his voice, talent and image remain instantly recognizable around the world.

Long live the King, and long may he continue to reign!

UK CHRISTMAS NUMBER ONES 1952-2022

1963

I WANT TO HOLD YOUR HAND/ THIS BOY
THE BEATLES

Four young men from Liverpool turned the music world inside out. John, Paul, George and Ringo - Yeh, yeh, yeh! This Christmas chart topper was their fourth single and their first to be recorded using four tracks. The single was the fastest selling title in British history, and when later issued in America, passed sales of 1.8 million, with eventual global sales of 15 million copies.

John Winston Lennon was born 9 October 1940 (died 8 December 1980). When his father left the household, his mother remarried, leaving Lennon to be raised by his Aunt Mimi and her husband George. James Paul McCartney was born 18 June 1942. His mother died from breast cancer. His father bought him his first guitar then taught him to play it. George Harrison was born 24 February 1943 (died 29 November 2001) and Richard "Ringo Starr" Starkey was born 7 July 1940.

John Lennon formed the skiffle quartet The Quarry Men and recruited Paul McCartney as a member. Paul introduced George Harrison and Stuart Sutcliffe joined as the fourth guitarist with Pete Best as drummer. They changed their name from The Silver Beatles to The Beatles. As such they toured locally, were regular performers at Liverpool's The Cavern Club, before gigging in Hamburg and Germany, building up a solid following. While in Hamburg for a second trip, The Beatles met Bert Kaempfert, a West German orchestra leader, and record producer for Polydor Records. While there he hired them to back Tony Sheridan in the studio, where they recorded "My Bonnie", "When The Saints Go Marching In", "Ain't She Sweet" and "Cry For A Shadow". The first two songs were released as a single.

Back in Liverpool, Brian Epstein managed a thriving record shop NEMS (North End Road Music Store) and he was constantly asked for the "My Bonnie" single by Tony Sheridan and The Beat Brothers. His curiosity led him to The Cavern Club to watch The Beatles perform. In December 1961 he became the group's manager, and as he was familiar with the workings of record companies through his retail business, distributed demo tapes to the major companies in London, including EMI Records. They turned down the group, although Decca Records offered them an audition. It was unsuccessful.

Brian Epstein would not admit defeat, and through sheer determination met George Martin, A&R manager for the EMI Records' subsidiary label Parlophone. Martin agreed to produce a recording session with the group at Abbey Road Studios in North London. One of the songs played was "Love Me Do", a Lennon/McCartney original composition. George Martin insisted that Pete Best be replaced as drummer, whereupon Ringo Starr, from Rory Storm and the Hurricanes, joined the group.

"Love Me Do", with John Lennon playing harmonica in the style of Bruce Channel's "Hey Baby", was issued in October 1962. Seven days later The Beatles were support act for Little Richard at New Brighton's Tower Ballroom. The Beatles' debut single hit the UK top twenty. The follow-up "Please Please Me" released early 1963 was a number two hit; the single was also the name of the group's debut album which went on to spend thirty consecutive weeks in pole position. It was replaced by their second album "With The Beatles". In between singles, they continued to tour the UK and make regular appearances at The Cavern Club. In constant demand for television and radio dates, The Beatles could be seen and heard all over the UK. And while they were promoting their product, Brian Epstein was negotiating an American recording deal.

By the release of their third single "She Loves You", Beatlemania had made its presence felt. Their concerts were sold out and their music was barely audible over the screaming from devoted adolescent fans. Newspaper headlines glared with riotous conditions, leaving parents worried about the effects this musical revolution would have on their children. Now nicknamed "The Fab Four", the group was big business, thanks to their exhausting touring and promotional schedules. With advance orders of half a million, "She Loves You" hit the top spot and went on to sell 1.3 million copies. In November 1963 "With The Beatles" attracted 300,000 advance orders, followed by the group's first European tour. Upon their return to the UK, Heathrow Airport was under siege as screaming fans welcomed home their idols. They then appeared on the popular variety show "Sunday Night At The London Palladium", and later at the Royal Command Performance where their act is best remembered for John Lennon's remark – "will the people in the cheaper seats clap your hands, while the rest of you just rattle your jewellery".

"I Want To Hold Your Hand" was rush released during 1963, and with advanced orders of one million this time, it entered the singles chart at the top, where it stayed for five weeks. When the single was first released in the US, The Beatles were performing in Paris. They changed their plans, to fly from France to Kennedy Airport in New York for their first US visit, and when they landed on 7 February 1964 were greeted by screaming, hysterical teenagers. It was later confirmed to be a promotional ploy by their record company, EMI Records' North American outlet, Capitol Records, who announced on the radio that anyone who went to the airport would get a free t-shirt! Nonetheless, the noisy scenes reminded them of home. Led by "I Want To Hold Your Hand", The Beatles dominated the first five places in the US Hot 100 singles chart. Demand for their product was so intense that Capitol Records' pressing plant rented space in their competitors' factories. To capitalise, and to fuel, this remarkable success, The Beatles performed in New York's Paramount

Theatre, and Carnegie Hall, Washington's State Coliseum, Kansas City's Municipal Stadium and Cleveland's Public Auditorium. Among the television appearances, the group guested on the legendary "Ed Sullivan Show".

To cash in on The Beatles' American breakthrough single, the previously licensed "My Bonnie" was re-issued; when released in the UK, it was a top fifty hit.

"I Want To Hold Your Hand" enriched all those involved. Not only the group, or producer George Martin, but Brian Epstein who had worked so hard to break them in America, and, who after several false starts, persuaded Capitol Records to sign them. When The Beatles put Liverpool on the map, a raft of other local groups were signed to recording deals. like Cilla Black, Gerry and the Pacemakers, Billy J Kramer and the Dakotas, and The Merseybeats. Most enjoyed considerable chart success, marking the arrival of the Mersey Beat Explosion. However, unbeknown to anyone at the time, The Beatles' unprecedented success in America, was also the start of another invasion, this time the Brit one. Dusty Springfield was the artist to follow The Fab Four, with the Mersey Beat acts close behind, and the Dave Clark Five, The Searchers, The Animals, Manfred Mann, among others, hot on their heels.

And all because The Beatles wanted to hold somebody's hand!

(See also Christmas 1964, 1965 and 1967)

1964

I FEEL FINE/ SHE'S A WOMAN
THE BEATLES

After spearheading the British invasion of America, many of the acts that followed enjoyed US hits for the first time. The British were taking over, and not before time either. With their fringed pudding bowl haircuts, smart, collarless matching suits and ties, The Beatles, with their close-knit harmonies, were breaking away from the R&B influenced sound which they loved so much, to embrace mainstream music like they owned it.

As 1964 closed, The Beatles' fourth album "Beatles For Sale" was replaced by "A Hard Day's Night". The title track was the name of their next chart topping single, released as the follow-up to "Can't Buy Me Love", the first song to be played on the pirate station, Radio Caroline. It was also the title to the group's first film, shot in black and white, portraying a week of their life as recording stars. Wilfred Brambell, Norman Rossington, Lionel Blair and David Janson were among the guest performers. "A Hard Days' Night" was premiered on 6 July 1964 in London, grossing around £15,000 during its first week.

Written by John Lennon, although credited to both him and Paul McCartney, "I Feel Fine", featured the first use of guitar feedback on a single thanks to Lennon's growing love of music technology. This distorted introduction was the prototype for later rock acts like The Who and Jimi Hendrix. With advanced orders of 750,000 copies, the single was destined to top the Christmas chart, displacing The Rolling Stones' "Little Red Rooster". Dominating the UK chart for five weeks, "I Feel Fine" was released simultaneously in the UK and US. The single sold over one million copies in the UK alone. When released in America, the song passed gold status, but attracted controversy, as it bore a resemblance to Bobby Parker's "Watch Your Step" recorded four years earlier. Following the release of the Christmas number one, plans were put in line for the group to film their second film "Help!"

The Beatles were British, but they were also global superstars; their talent to produce multi-million selling music seemed unshakeable. Every note they recorded turned to gold. They lacked nothing materially. Money was abundant, beyond their dreams, and they worked non-stop. The Beatles had no private lives. Every moment was recorded and printed, and whether they liked it or not, they were becoming British ambassadors abroad, and integral members of the British Establishment.

1965 started with the Christmas chart topper, and was followed by another two – "Ticket To Ride" and "Help!". Shortly after the release of the latter, it was announced The Beatles would each receive the MBE, to be presented during a ceremony held in October 1965. Apparently, the group smoked marijuana in the Palace, having smuggled it in, hidden away in John Lennon's boots! Honouring the group in this way annoyed Colonel Frederick Wragg sufficiently, who in protest returned 12 medals, while the Canadian politician Hector Dupuis himself an MBE recipient, dubbed The Beatles 'vulgar numbskulls'.

Also in 1965, "The Beatles (Invite You To Take A Ticket To Ride)" was the final in a series of BBC Radio's Bank Holiday specials broadcast in June. John Lennon published his second book, "A Spaniard In The Works" – the first being "In His Own Write", and received countless awards and honours in recognition of their record sales. One being presented to Paul McCartney at the Ivor Novello Awards ceremony for Highest Certified British Sales and Most Performed Work (1964) for "Can't Buy Me Love".

For the time being, The Beatles had no equal.

(See also Christmas 1963, 1965 and 1967)

1965

DAY TRIPPER/ WE CAN WORK IT OUT
THE BEATLES

This Christmas chart topper marked the end of the three year run for The Fab Four. A double header, it also shot to the top of the international charts, including America where it was the group's 11th number one. Written in haste during the recording sessions for their next album "Rubber Soul", it was inspired by Bobby Parker's guitar riff in his 1961 single "Watch Your Step". As nobody could decide which track to issue as the top side – John Lennon wanted "Day Tripper", while Paul McCartney and others insisted on "We Can Work It Out", a double A sided single was the fairest option.

Prior to the release of the Christmas single, The Beatles starred in their second film "Help", inspired by the Marx Brothers and starring Leo McKern, Eleanor Bron, Roy Kinnear and Patrick Cargill, Shot in colour it was a comedy adventure where the group fought - with lots of running - an evil cult. The film premiered in August 1965 and grossed over £10,000. "Help" the single, topped the UK chart the same month, followed by the film soundtrack.

The Beatles then toured the US again, opening at the Shea Stadium, New York, breaking box office records. It was during this tour that The Beatles met Elvis Presley at his Bel Air Mansion.

The Beatles were now regular users of the drug LSD, introduced to them by a dentist they met at a dinner party. To close 1965, they toured the UK for the last time, while a television tribute "The Music Of Lennon/McCartney" was screened, starring artists like Cilla Black, Billy J Kramer and Peter Sellers. The Beatles previewed "We Can Work It Out", the song that symbolised McCartney's optimism and Lennon's pessimism. A perfect combination.

It was the group's ninth number one single. The song has since been recorded by a host of artists including Otis Redding, Valerie Simpson, Chaka Khan, The Four Seasons, Nancy Sinatra, and Stevie Wonder, who went one step further and performed the song live for Paul McCartney at the 1990 Grammy Lifetime Award ceremony.

John Lennon and Paul McCartney had been in-demand as writers since the group became famous. Very few acts would record a Beatles' original – commercial suicide – but some did reap success. The UK folk outfit The

Overlanders were one with their version of the album track "Michelle" from the "Rubber Soul" album. That same song also provided a US hit for the alter egos of the UK songwriting/producing production unit, David and Jonathan.

The Beatles were at the top of their game

(See also Christmas 1963, 1964 and 1967)

1966

GREEN GRASS OF HOME/ PROMISE HER ANYTHING
TOM JONES

This year's Christmas number one emulated a style of music with which this artist would achieve global success. Yes, the man born Thomas Jones Woodward in Pontypridd, Wales on 7 June 1940, was on his way to becoming a superstar and this Christmas single was his second to hit the pole position.

From a young age, Thomas pursued his singing ambitions. His first professional debut was in 1957 at The Treforest Working Men's Club, Glamorgan. Then he formed his first group, Tommy Scott and the Senators to record for EMI Records in 1963. It was an unsuccessful relationship. However, while performing in Pontypridd, he was spotted by Gordon Mills, who worked for Leeds Music. He was impressed by what he saw and offered Thomas a management contract. After changing his name to Tom Jones (from the film of the same name), Gordon Mills secured him a deal with Decca Records. His first single was the Ronnie Love's hit "Chills And Fever" which flopped. Powerful-voiced Jones was strongly influenced by American rock, and soul music; in particular Elvis Presley, and artists from companies like Motown, Stax and Chess. However, his strong voice was more reminiscent of traditional vocalists like Paul Robeson, Howard Keel and Frankie Laine.

Tom's second single, "It's Not Unusual" written initially for Sandie Shaw. While she pondered whether to record it or not, Tom released his version to top the UK chart in 1965. The single also hit the US top ten, and because the Americans believed him to be an African-American, the title became an R&B hit also. With the UK hit to his credit, Tom Jones hired the backing group The Squires for their first live performance at the annual "New Musical Express" concert staged in London, and also guest on television's top variety show, Sunday Night At The London Palladium. "Once Upon A Time" followed his chart topper, but was a poor selling release. Nonetheless, he embarked upon his first major British tour, and due to his American success appeared twice on The Ed Sullivan Show, guested at the Paramount Theatre in New York, and the Brooklyn Fox Theatre where he joined Murray The K's gala concert.

"With These Hands" was next, but it was "What's New Pussycat", the theme song from the film of the same name, that returned him to the upper rungs of the UK chart. It also hit the US top three, prompting him to capitalise on his success by touring there. By the end of 1965, Tom had recorded another film theme "Promise Her Anything" and hosted his first UK television show, Call In Tom. This was followed by others, like This Is Tom Jones (1969 – 1970) and Tom Jones (1980 – 1981). He started 1966 as the winner in the Best New Artist 1965 category at the eighth annual Grammy Awards ceremony and recorded the title track from the fourth James Bond film, Thunderball. "Not Responsible" and "This And That" followed but it was during December that he was re-established as a top selling artist when he covered Jerry Lee Lewis' "Green Green Grass Of Home". The single topped the chart for seven weeks, selling in excess of a million copies. Decca Records' first and Tom Jones' biggest selling single ever. The song has its roots in American country music. Before Tom Jones' version, it was a country/western smash for Portener Wagoner, while Jerry Lee Lewis' take had yet to reach British soil.

Tom Jones became a leading male sex symbol for the remainder of the 1960s (and beyond, some will argue). With a visual mixture of dark curly hair, hairy chest and a commanding Welsh voice, it was understable. In retrospect he was more likely to appeal to the housewife/young woman record buyers, than teenage girls, although in later years he crossed over all barriers.

In 1967 Tom toured South America, released "Detroit City" as the chart topper's follow up to become a UK top ten hit. Alongside his many American commitments, he performed at London's top nighterie Talk Of The Town, and released a further two singles "I'll Never Fall In Love Again" and "I'm Coming Home". A year later he released the singalong "Delilah", "Help Yourself" and "A Minute Of Your Time" in between Las Vegas performances.

Early into the 1970s he continued to chart with singles like "Without Love (There Is Nothing)", "I (Who Have Nothing)", "She's A Lady", "Puppet Man" and "Till" , while most of his touring was concentrated in America, where he broke box office records at New York's Madison Square Gardens by selling $350,000 worth of tickets. By now, Tom was one of the highest paid singers in the world, and as the bulk of his wealth was in dollars, he relocated to California in 1975. Two years later, he scored his first legitimate US country number one hit with "Say You'll Stay Until Tomorrow". Then, when signed directly to Mercury Records' Country Music Division, he scored 13 country chart singles (including a remake of "Green Green Grass Of Home" as the flip to "Things That Matter Most To Me"), over a four year period.

After a decade's hiatus in America, Tom Jones decided to head back to the UK to promote the soundtrack to the musical Matador in which he had a featured song titled "A Boy From Nowhere". Recorded in his original middle of the road style, the single (released by Epic Records) peaked at number two in 1987, signalling the first of his several comebacks during the next twenty years. In 1988, after singing Prince's "Kiss" on the TV programme The Last Resort hosted by Jonathan Ross, the instrumental group, Art Of Noise, persuaded him to be lead vocalist on their version of the song. The single was a UK top five / US top forty hit on the China Records imprint, whereupon Tom signed a recording contract with Jive Records, where his only album for the label "At This Moment" was issued in 1989. A version of Phyllis Nelson's "Move Closer" was extracted as a single to reach the UK top fifty. At the end of the year, he released the album "After Dark" for compilation specialists

Stylus Records which, thanks to television advertising, peaked in the UK top fifty. He also received a star on the Hollywood Walk Of Fame, cementing his popularity in America.

It is interesting to note that Tom's original manager Gordon Mills, also had Engelbert Humperdinck and Gilbert O'Sullivan on his books. Engelbert and Tom were, to all intents and purposes, identical middle of the road ballad crooners vying for the same market. Only Tom Jones, however, managed to be successfully consistent across the decades to have a presence in every or every alternate year on either the UK single or album charts. Just like some of his contemporaries - Cliff Richard, Lulu and Status Quo - Tom Jones has definitely that certain something to keeps him in the public eye. In 1997 he recorded "You Can Leave Your Hat On" for the soundtrack of The Full Monty film, and two years later, recorded "Sex Bomb" in collaboration with Mousse T - a number three UK hit, and the biggest selling track from his "Reload" album. Also in 1999 he was awarded an OBE, and a knighthood from the Queen in 2006 for services to music. Throughout his career he has received countless honours, including the Best New Artist 1966 Grammy Award, and two BRIT awards, for Best British Male in 2000, and three years later, Outstanding Contribution To Music.

In 2007 Tom joined invited artists to perform at The Concert For Diana at London's Wembley Stadium, and the next year recorded his first album of new material for fifteen years. Titled "24 Hours" it was released by S-Curve Records. In 2009 he contributed to "Islands In The Stream", a cover version of the Bee Gees' original. The single hit the pole position, raising funds for Comic Relief. Album-wise he reached number two with this thirty-ninth studio album, the blues/gospel infused "Praise And Blame" project, for Island Records in 2010, and the similar styled "Spirit In The Room" became a top ten hit two years later, the 2015 issued "Long Lost Suitcase" (released on Virgin) - his 40th studio album was another respectable album seller.

Six years later he released his most recent studio project, the musically organic and eclectic "Surrounded By Time" which debuted at number one on the UK Albums chart - his fourth number one UK album in his career.

A man now aged in his mid-eighties, Tom Jones wears his hair a natural grey, and his lifestyle has mellowed and matured. It is fifty years or so since he has been the star attraction before capacity filled venues of screaming girls who threw their panties and house keys on stage in the hope that he would respond. But his presence is just as commanding, and his voice as strong. As a senior, he was one of the original judges on BBC1's reality show The Voice where his advice was invaluable to hopefuls. Tom was married to the same lady Melinda since 1957 despite his several high profile affairs with The Supremes' Mary Wilson, among others. Melinda Woodward - also known as 'Linda' - died on 10 April 2016 at Cedars Sinai Hospital in Los Angeles after losing a battle with cancer, leading Tom to cancel numerous concert engagements.

Tom Jones is a true British musical institution, who has celebrated successes as well as riding the flops. To date, he has enjoyed 36 UK top forty hits and 19 US hits. We are all awaiting his next move.

UK CHRISTMAS NUMBER ONES 1952-2022

1967

HELLO GOODBYE/ I AM THE WALRUS
THE BEATLES

Credited to Lennon and McCartney this Christmas chart topper was in fact penned by solo Paul. It was a song about everything and nothing, but represented several changes in the group. Gone were the pudding bowl haircuts and smart suits, and their clean cut image. Still heavily into LSD, they had starred in a badly organised film "Magical Mystery Tour" and sought solace in the teachings of Maharishi Mahesh Yogi.

During 1966, while they had no musical equal, The Beatles could not rely totally on public support. In May they performed in London for the last time, and a month later were escorted through the streets of Hamburg; their first visit since 1963. They then performed in Tokyo, Japan. Their first UK chart topper of the year was "Paperback Writer". The trade advertising and packaging for this single caused a huge uproar, as it pictured the group wearing white overalls, holding dismembered dolls and slices of raw meat. Both were changed. "Yelllow Submarine"/"Eleanor Rigby" was next, with "Penny Lane"/"Strawberry Fields Forever" following: another double headed release.

However in mid-1967 The Beatles excelled themselves. With their eighth studio album, they altered the course of music. Titled "Sgt Pepper's Lonely Hearts Club Band", it was classed as a musical masterpiece, a musical innovation and revolution, and the most influential rock 'n' roll album ever released. It inspired and educated, and proved beyond doubt The Beatles were creative artists and not just performers. Selling 30 million copies, the album knew no bounds. Today, it is still considered an iconic release that shaped future music. A month after the release of "Sgt Pepper's Lonely Hearts Club Band" in July, The Beatles topped the UK chart once more with "All You Need Is Love" first aired on the BBC TV programme "Our World" as part of a global link up. A month later, amid all the success came tragedy when the group's manager Brian Epstein committed suicide. He was 32 years old. The Beatles were devastated when the news was broken to them during their stay with the Maharishi Mahesh Yogi in North Wales. The group would survive without him although maybe not in the manner he would have envisaged.

"Hello Goodbye" topped the UK singles chart for seven weeks (equalling the stay by "From Me To You") and was the group's 15th US chart topper. John Lennon was not impressed that this childish song could sell in such vast quantities, much preferring the more adult flipside. The single's promotional video could not be screened by BBC TV because the Musicians Union had banned miming to songs on television. After several attempts to get round the decision, the single was promoted with snippets from the film "A Hard Day's Night". Both songs were featured in "The Magical Mystery Tour" film, soundtrack and EP, where 43 people including an oversized lady, a midget, a few journalists and loads of extras joined The Beatles on a coach ride. Left to their own devices, the film was cluttered and confusing, and the project flopped. In later years, it attracted a huge cult following and was a valued addition to their fans' collections.

Also in 1967 The Beatles opened Apple, their own boutique at London's 94 Baker Street (it was the place for beautiful people), Apple Tailoring at 161 New King's Road, and, a year later, in line with their EMI Records' contract, opened up Apple Records, as an outlet for artists signed to the new label. Welsh songstress Mary Hopkin was one of the most successful acts. The label was a subsidiary of the parent company, Apple Corps Ltd, based in 3 Savile Row, London. And it was also the year that the group was hounded by the police searching for drugs, and when the empire they had built began to splinter. The final singles of 1968 were both chart toppers - "Lady Madonna", the last to be issued on EMI's Parlophone label, and "Hey Jude" the first to carry the new Apple logo which was licensed to EMI for manufacture and distribution. Two further singles hit the top spot before the end of the decade – "Get Back" and "The Ballad Of John And Yoko" (featuring Lennon's future second wife Yoko Ono). Three albums were also released – "The Beatles (White Album)" so called because the packaging was entirely white and free from lettering; "Yellow Submarine", and "Abbey Road". The Beatles had performed together for the last time, and would star in one more film together.

As the 1970s loomed, The Beatles were growing as individuals, planning a future that would pre-empt the group fracturing further. To this end, the Apple boutique was closed and the stock given away. John Lennon formed the Plastic Ono Band; George Harrison wrote and sang "Something" (a number two UK hit); Ringo Starr appeared in the film "Candy", and Paul McCartney formed the nucleus of Wings. But fracture the group did with businessman's Allen Klein's help. Hired by Lennon, the intention was for Klein to sort out the tangled business knot created by the group.

But still they recorded. "Get Back" later re-titled "Let It Be" was the title of their 12th and final album; with a single and film bearing the same title. The film included the group's unannounced performance on the roof of their Savile Row offices, and footage in the recording studio, while the album was recorded under fraught conditions and included keyboardist Billy Preston.

In December 1970 when Paul McCartney dissolved The Beatles, the party was over; the last curtain fell on a musical era. Each Beatle pursued a solo recording career, while repeated re-issued albums and compilations added to their individual earning power.

On 8 December 1980 John Lennon was gunned down by Mark Chapman, a crazed fan, outside of his home at Dakota Buildings in New York. He had just returned from the Record Plant Studio, with his wife Yoko Ono. On 29 November 2001 George Harrison died from cancer in Los Angeles, California.

Of the many Beatles' recordings available since the untimely death of John and George, one of the most valued was the discovery of two Lennon songs: the 1977 demo "Free As A Bird", and "Real Love" - both UK top five hits in 1995. In 2010, EMI Records re-mastered the "red" and "blue" "Greatest Hits" albums which spanned 1962-1967, and 1967-1970 respectively. Both entered the top ten UK chart, with availability on iTunes.

Two years on from that event, EMI Records reissued the complete Beatles album back catalogue on vinyl. In 2013 Universal Music merged/acquired and restructured EMI's recorded music operations but for the deal to be concluded and agreed by the European Union, both Universal and EMI were required to sell a number of their imprints and interests including Parlophone Records – which would be entirely sold lock, stock and barrel to rival music giants Warner Music . However as a 'sweetener' the newly proposed 'Universal EMI Music' would retain the rights to the Beatles' entire back catalogue as well as the entire solo back catalogue recordings of all four Beatles members, the revived Capitol Records UK imprint of the new Universal EMI Music will now be the new outlet for all Beatles related product, with the slight change of hands of recording home it is unlikely to change the fact that the Apple logo will sometimes be used.

The Beatles are still big business. Their home town of Liverpool has dedicated itself to their memory with museums, memorabilia, galleries and a re-structured Cavern Club. Books about their music, biographies, lyrics, tours, etc, are written with great regularity.

Musically the rediscoveries reared their heads once again in late 2023 Dubbed "the last Beatles song", "Now and Then". Based around a John Lennon recorded demo from the late 1970s, was released on 2 November 2023 and served as a taster for yet another planned Beatles compilation retrospective in time for the Christmas sales market.

That little Apple logo still packs a powerful punch!

George Martin died in his sleep on the night of 8 March 2016 at his Wiltshire home at the age of 90 of natural causes. Ringo Starr and Universal Music both confirmed his death. He is survived by his wife Judy Lockhart Smith and his four children – another closing chapter to the Beatles heritage

(See also Christmas 1963, 1964 and 1965)

UK CHRISTMAS NUMBER ONES 1952-2022

1968

LILY THE PINK/ BUTTONS OF YOUR MIND
SCAFFOLD

Written by all three band members, Roger McGough, Mike McGear and John Gorman, "Lily The Pink" was the ideal Christmas number one, because if ever there was a perfect party song, this was it! The Liverpool trio performed poetry and stand up comedy with music across the country, notably in London, Edinburgh and regularly at Liverpool's Everyman Theatre. Their popularity escalated as the public flocked to see their unique brand of entertainment.

Mike McGear (real name Peter Michael McCartney) is Paul McCartney's younger brother, and acknowledged that Scaffold was the prototype for Monty Python, and perhaps there is truth to that statement because the UK had rarely heard this type of comedy on disc. Although the public was aware of the connection between McGear and McCartney, and the fact that Scaffold was signed to EMI Records' Parlophone label, the same as The Beatles, it was hard to believe Paul had no further musical involvement in their recording deal. He did, but as an inspiration, because he gave his brother a camera which inspired the trio's first charting single "Thank U Very Much" which was a top ten single in December 1967. Prior to this, Scaffold had issued two other poor selling singles – "2 Days Monday" and "Goodbat Nightman".

However, Scaffold's biggest hit dominated the top spot for two separate two-week runs, spending a total of 24 weeks on the chart. Is it the case that anything goes when it comes to Christmas, or perhaps, that the British record buying public couldn't get a big enough dose of musical tomfoolery? We're not sure, but the music hall styled "Lily The Pink" was proven to be their biggest ever hit, with it's pub-style piano and nonsense lyrics which tickled the public. Yet the song did have a serious side which many missed. It was inspired by Lydia Pinkham, born in 1819 in Massachusetts, who developed a woman's tonic to relieve the symptoms of menstrual cycles and the menopause. Revisit the lyrics – "For she invented medicinal compound. Most efficacious in every case". The sound was very British, directed at the unique sense of humour, which was clearly proven when it bombed in America. In fairness, the single was a one off, and no amount of musical cloning could change that.

Incidentally backing personnel on the Norrie Paramor produced version included a (pre-fame) Elton John, Tim Rice as well as Cream's Jack Bruce and the Hollies / Crosby, Stills, Nash & Young alumni Graham Nash

UK CHRISTMAS NUMBER ONES 1952-2022

A year to the month, the chart topper's follow-up was released. Another unusual release as it was a version of the Scouts' tune 'Gin Gan Goolie' which peaked in the top forty, but spent 12 weeks on chart. Perhaps forseeing the end was in sight for Scaffold, the membership took a sabbatical with Mike McGear embarking upon a solo career to record "Woman", while Roger McGough concentrated on his poetry. In 1970, the re-formed Scaffold hosted Score With The Scaffold, a children's television series, and two years later produced the music film Plod shot in Liverpool. In 1973, the trio signed a deal with Island Records to issue an album "Fresh Liver", then moved to Warner Brothers to release the Paul McCartney-produced single "Liverpool Lou" – a top ten hit in June 1974. The parent album "Sold Out" flopped as did a move two years later to the Bronze Records label, forcing the trio to lay Scaffold to rest, and for Mike McGear to attempt another solo career. This time it resulted in a UK top forty entrant with "Leave It".

John Gorman went on to join the cast of Saturday morning children's show Tiswas, and was a member of that programme's spin-off music group The Four Bucketeers, who scored a 1980 hit on CBS Records with "The Bucket Of Water Song" - slightly reminiscent in places to "Lily The Pink". In 2006 Mike McGear, who by now also became a successful photographer, found himself in the news when he was cleared of groping a young waitress in a bar, and later campaigning to push an anonymity law through Parliament for people accused, but not proved guilty of, serious crimes.

Every now and again Scaffold reform; in 2010 for a gala in Shanghai, to celebrate the of the Liverpool Pavilion's role in the World Expo.

In 2020, all three original members of the Scaffold released a re-worked version of their 1967 hit "Thank U Very Much" in support of the NHS during the COVID-19 pandemic.

UK CHRISTMAS NUMBER ONES 1952-2022

1969

TWO LITTLE BOYS/ I LOVE MY LOVE
ROLF HARRIS

Achieving the distinction of being the last ever UK number one single of the 1960s and first of the 1970s, Rolf Harris perhaps set the style and tone for the laid back pop style of the early seventies. EMI Records released "Two Little Boys" which ended the eight week reign of American cartoon pop group The Archies, when their sweet and bubbly "Sugar Sugar" single was replaced by the solemn, yet perhaps tongue-n-cheek style, of Rolf Harris's song, telling the story of a wartime friendship. The title reached the top twenty on the US Adult Contemporary chart.

Born in Wembley Park, Perth, Australia in March 1930, Rolf Harris became a world class entertainer, painter, television personality and singer. He was educated at the Perth Modern School and the University of Western Australia. As a teenager, he painted in oils; his self portrait was hung in the Art Gallery of New South Wales. He also received other honours for his work, and it was a talent he nurtured as he grew older. He was also a champion swimmer from 1948 to 1952.

Having moved to the UK in 1955, he studied at the City and Guilds Art School, Kensington, London. In 1953, he had secured a ten-minute slot on a BBC TV programme Jigsaw with a puppet named Fuzz. Within a year, he was a regular guest on Whirligig with his own creation Willoughby who lived on his drawing board. During the 1960s he presented Hi There! And Hey Presto It's Rolf, before hosting his own series The Rolf Harris Show for seven years. In the 1980s he was a popular television guest where he painted pictures on large boards with decorating brushes in a slapdash, colourful fashion, asking while he painted – "can you tell what it is yet?" He had his own programmes Rolf Harris' Cartoon Time and Rolf's Cartoon Club through to the 1990s. Animal Hospital, a thirty-minute look into the daily routine of a London PDSA surgery, and Rolf On Art (which featured his 80th birthday portrait of Queen Elizabeth) are just two of the television programmes that enjoyed peak time screenings through the 1990s.

Alongside his television career, Rolf Harris also became a successful singer. Before Kylie Minogue's arrival in the late 1980s, he was Britain's most successful Australian born chart act. He also enjoyed US success with his debut UK hit "Tie Me Kangeroo Down Sport" first released in 1960 but not charting in the USA until three years later.

"Sun Arise" in October 1962 was his next hit, with "Johnny Day" a year later, and "Bluer Than Blue", six years' later. As "Jake The Peg" was one of his highlights on stage, it was issued as the flipside to "Big Dog". It flopped, but as audiences continued to love seeing him strut across the stage with his extra leg, he kept it in his act.

Novelty and straight songs formed the basis of Rolf's singing career, although he harboured an ambition to sing rock and roll. To this end he did just that, by recording Led Zeppelin's "Stairway To Heaven" and Queen's "Bohemian Rhapsody" in 1993 and 1996 respectively. His last charting title, "Fine Day" was issued on the Tommy Boy label in 2000.

Whether television host, personality, artist or singer, Rolf Harris has certainly made his mark. In 2010 he appeared as a performer at the Ise of Wight's Bestival Festival, later at Glastonbury, and a year later, he performed at the Wickham Festival in Hampshire. In 2011, the Fine Art Trade Guild honoured him as the Best Selling Published Artist of the year, and during 2012, his paintings exhibition "Rolf Harris: Can You Tell What It Is Yet?" was held at Liverpool's Walker Art Gallery.

Rolf Harris was headline news again in 2013, this time due to the ongoing 'Yewtree' investigations by the Metropolitan Police Service started in October 2012 relating to celebrity sex abuse crimes, notably spearheaded by crimes conducted by media personality and charity fundraiser Jimmy Saville, who died in October 2011. The police investigations began following an ITV documentary titled "Exposure: The Other Side Of Jimmy Saville" which led to investigations into others including television stars and other personalities. Rolf Harris was found guilty on 12 charges of indecent assault between 1969 – 1986, and was sentenced to five years and nine months.

The ultimate rise and fall of a household name.

In May 2023, Harris died at his Berkshire home in Bray, Berkshire at the age of 93.

UK CHRISTMAS NUMBER ONES 1952-2022

1970

I HEAR YOU KNOCKING/ BLACK BILL
DAVE EDMUNDS

A Welshman's cover version of an obscure R&B song became the Christmas number one hit for 1970. New Orleans musician Smiley Lewis and his wife Pearl King wrote the song, but Smiley was deprived of a major hit single because a 'whitewashed' version became a US pop hit for Gale Storm. The song was a relatively unknown to the rest of the world until a US promotional tour undertaken by Dave Edmunds changed all that.

Born in April 1944, in Cardiff, Wales, Edmunds learned to play the guitar at school, where he joined his first group, The 99ers. He then switched to The Raiders, before moving to London in 1966 to join The Image. This in time led to him forming a trio with guitarist John Williams and Image's drummer, Tommy Riley. They were signed to EMI Records, changed their name to The Human Beans and their first single "Morning Dew" was issued in June 1967. Then Love Sculpture was born, and after a depressing start, scored a 1968 UK top five hit with a frantic version of "Sabre Dance". The group was a one hit wonder, and later disbanded, leaving Dave Edmunds to pursue a solo career as a singer/producer for his newly opened Rockfield recording studios based in Monmouth, Wales. Among other things, he intended to produce emerging talent signed to Rockfield in a classic R&B/rock style, but that was to change when during a promotional trip to America, he first heard what would become his biggest selling chart single. He originally planned to record Wilbert Harrison's "Let's Work Together", but those plans were dropped when American blues-rock band Canned Heat scored a UK number hit with it during the start of 1970. Hence, the cue for reworking "I Hear You Knocking".

Signed to Gordon Mills' MAM agency, his single was issued on its offshoot label to sell over three million copies, securing the top spot for Christmas (and reaching the US top 5 along the way). On the back of this success, EMI Records signed him for a follow up single and an album, but both "I'm Coming Home" and "Rockpile" failed to register. However, both managed to ripple the US charts.

With a change of style and yet another label change, it took just over two years for Edmunds to re-establish himself as a chart act. He secured a deal for his Rockfield label with RCA Records, to score two UK top 10 hits with cover versions of The Ronettes' "Baby I Love You" and The Chordettes' "Born To Be

With You", both ditching the R&B/rock slant of old, for a Phil Spector inspired sound. By the late 1970s, the R&B/rock sound that Edmunds started out with re-appeared. It was updated with a heavy musical slant towards American country music. In 1977, Edmunds introduced his new group Rockpile to the world, for a fresh run of hits, this time via the Atlantic/WEA distributed Swan Song imprint (Led Zeppelin's label). Rockpile's membership included Nick Lowe, whose penned "I Knew The Bride" was a top thirty hit. This success led to Edmunds being active as a touring act, notably playing on Lowe's tour for Stiff Records, and a US package tour alongside new wave acts Elvis Costello and Mink De Ville. In fact, Elvis Costello provided Edmunds with his biggest hit single for some time: "Girls Talk", which reached the UK top five, and US top seventy in 1979. He then closed the 1970s with his final British top twenty single, titled "Queen Of Hearts", which later became an American top ten hit for female country rocker Juice Newton. During the next decade, he enjoyed further mid-selling singles like "Singing The Blues", "Almost Saturday Night" and "The Race Is On!" (with The Stray Cats).

Dave Edmunds continued to record into the 1990s, but with every decreasing chart position he concentrated more on production for other artists including Status Quo, Dion, The Everly Brothers, and Shakin' Stevens. He also remixed Kim Wilde's 1985 comeback hit "Rage To Love" for single release. Although no longer a chart name of note, Dave Edmunds continues to work in the changing music business, with public appearance now and again.

UK CHRISTMAS NUMBER ONES 1952-2022

1971

ERNIE (THE FASTEST MILKMAN IN THE WEST)/ TING-A-LING-A-LOO
BENNY HILL

It was a decade that started with the hangover of 1960s flower power, and closing with both the mirror ball and safety pin representing the changing youth culture. In between the paisley shirts and pogo dancing there were the oddities of novelty pop singles in the UK charts. Some from the USA like, "The Streak", "Telephone Man", and "Disco Duck". The bulk, however, came from the UK, notably with releases from Lieutenant Pigeon, Judge Dread, Clive Dunn, The Wurzels and the man who dominated the UK chart over Christmas 1971. Silly season or not, Benny Hill's single knocked Slade off the top spot, and relegated T Rex into the 'almost there' position. The 1970s was THE decade for the novelty single!

Born in Southampton in January 1924 as Alfred Hawthorne Hill, Benny rechristened himself because he felt the original abbreviation of 'Alf Hill' sounded 'too Cockney'. His biggest hit as a recording artist was inspired by his teenage employment as a milkman who worked with a horse and cart. In the mid 1950s he recorded the self penned Country and Western pastiche "Ernie (The Fastest Milkman In the West)" but it wasn't the version that would be a top selling Christmas song some fifteen years later.

Determined to find work in the entertainment business, Benny Hill first worked as a stage manager with a touring company, before being drafted into the Armed Forces in 1942. He trained as a mechanic but joined the entertainments division where he made a name for himself. Once discharged, he embarked upon a career in music halls as a stand up comedian, paying tribute to Jack Benny, his inspiration. This led to him being a radio performer, before his first television appearance in 1950. He played different characters in a sitcom television series Benny Hill, won the role of Nick Bottom in the television production of A Midsummer Night's Dream, and hosted a successful radio run with Benny Hill Time until the mid-1960s.

Pye Records' producer and A&R man, Tony Hatch took a chance with Hill in the early 1960s and signed him to release a trio of singles - "Gather In The Mushrooms", "Transistor Radio" and "Harvest Of Love" – all charting titles between 1961 – 1963.

The Benny Hill Show was one of television's top entertainment programmes throughout the 1970s and 1980s. The short comedy sketch based show combined mime, slapstick and loads of double entendre, where Benny portrayed several characters, like Fred Scuttle, alongside regulars who included Bob Todd, Rita Webb, Patricia Hayes and Henry McGee. Recording stars of the time also guested, The Springfields, Alma Cogan and Petula Clark, among them. The Benny Hill Show spanned over thirty years, with 21 million people watching it at its peak.

With Benny Hill's style of risqué, non politically correct, humour becoming the order of the era, recording a novelty single was an obvious move. Eight years after his last single, Benny returned to the singles chart with his re-recording of "Ernie (The Fastest Milkman In The West)".

In the 1980s, when degrading humour, whether sexist or racist, was seen as old fashioned by the new guard of 'alternative' comedians, Benny Hill's brand of head-slapping, semi-naked girls in Keystone Cops chase scenes, slapstick humour, was an immediate casualty. And to make matters worse, his long running television show was dropped by Thames Television in 1989. A Thames Television executive told him the show was losing viewers and he was looking ill. Hard to swallow for Hill, because the series was still popular viewing in the UK, across the Continent, and in America, where he became a cult figure.

After Thames Television's decision to drop him from their broadcast schedules, Benny became a reclusive figure, and spent most of his days at his Middlesex home. In April 1992 he suffered a mild heart attack; a bypass was recommended but he refused treatment. Then his kidneys failed which contributed to his death in April 1992. Benny's body was discovered sitting in an armchair in front of his television set. The official cause of death was coronary thrombosis, although many believed he died from a broken heart following the loss of his television career. He was buried in Southampton.

Following Benny's death, EMI Records re-released "Ernie (The Fastest Milkman In The West)" although it failed to repeat its chart topping peak, twenty years earlier; becoming a modest top thirty hit instead.

Benny Hill is still considered by many to be British comedy royalty and that is unlikely to ever change.

UK CHRISTMAS NUMBER ONES 1952-2022

1972

LONG HAIRED LOVER FROM LIVERPOOL/ MOTHER OF MINE
LITTLE JIMMY OSMOND

This year's number one came from a very unlikely source. He was the youngest member of a superstar American singing family known for their toothy grins, barbershop harmonies and Mormon beliefs. Their musical blend of bubblegum, country and soul music, captured the world's imagination. The single itself was twee to say the least, and, some believed because of this, it was best forgotten. Indeed, it isn't often featured on 'oldie' stations like Capital Gold, or a 'must have' on 1970s' themed compilations. But someone must have liked it in 1972 because it dominated the UK top spot for five long weeks! The Osmonds were one of the top selling teen targeted acts in the world during the first half of the 1970s. In fact their closest competitors in this field were The Jackson 5 and David Cassidy from The Partridge Family. It was the era of international Osmond mania!

Born in April 1963, in Canoga Park, California (his siblings Alan, Wayne, Merrill, Jay, Donny, Marie, Virl and Tom, were born in Ogden, Utah) to George and Olive Osmond, James Arthur Osmond wasn't old enough to sing with Alan, Wayne, Merrill and Jay when they formed a barber shop quartet to perform locally in Ogden. Within a few years, as their popularity grew, their father arranged for them to audition for the television impresario Lawrence Welk, based in California. They were unsuccessful, so decided to visit Disneyland to cheer themselves up. This led to the brothers being hired to perform there, which, in turn, led to singer Andy Williams' father spotting them. He told his son how impressed was with their act, that they became regular attractions on The Andy Williams Show for seven years from 1962. They also toured with the singer. In 1969 they guested on The Jerry Lewis Show, where they decided they wanted to perform popular music. To this end, despite interest from Andy Williams's Barnaby label they secured a contract with MGM Records instead, with producer Mike Curb's help, to record "One Bad Apple" which hit the US top spot in 1971.

But it was in their 'bubblegum / blue eyed soul' phase where they found their musical niche with hits like "Crazy Horses" in 1972, "Going Home" , " I Can't Stop" and "Let Me In" up to their UK number one single in 1974 titled "Love Me For A Reason", a working of the Johnny Bristol original. By this time, Donny had a very successful solo career under his belt, while still a group member, likewise sister Marie with her 1973 hit "Paper Roses". So it was decided to let little Jimmy have a go. At the age of five he had already earned a gold disc for sales of "My Little Darling", recorded in Japanese, and was nine years old when his chirpy love song "Long Haired Lover From Liverpool" topped the UK chart over 1972's festive period. The British chart enjoyed – and endured – a phase of pre-teen singers dominating the early 1970s. Alongside the likes of Brit kids Neil Reid, Lena Zavaroni and Glyn Poole, a young American managed to do what they couldn't – hit the top spot with a confession that he had no idea where Liverpool was!

Jimmy's versions of "Tweedle Dee" and "I'm Gonna Knock On Your Door" in 1973 and 1974 respectively completed the trio of UK chart hits, although he continued to be a draw in Japan where he was affectionately known as 'Jimmy Boy'. Due to the exceptional family success across the world, which obviously played a major role in launching Jimmy as a solo artist, he returned to perform with his brothers until the group disbanded in 1980. At first they worked on the periphery of show business in various capacities: Jimmy, for example, became a respected impresario, helping to mastermind Michael Jackson's Bad world tour, and the proprietor of the Oz-Art advertising and design company. In 2005 Jimmy took part in the fifth series of the celebrity UK reality show I'm A Celebrity Get Me Out Of Here filmed in the Australian jungle where he came fourth. He has also appeared in several UK pantomimes, a touring company of Chicago, and guested on various television programmes, like Come Dine With Me and Celebrity Family Fortunes.

In time the brothers re-established themselves as entertainers across the world, including the UK, where Jimmy, Merrill and Jay perform as The Osmonds. One of their most recent performances was at Butlins, Bognor Regis, East Sussex, in September 2013 as part of a music weekender.

1973

MERRY XMAS EVERYBODY/ DON'T BLAME ME
SLADE

This single is as part of Christmas as turkey, snow and mince pies. A rare masterpiece that gets rolled out every twelve months - and to top it off, the song was written using discarded lyrics and music from other Slade songs, and recorded during a steaming hot summer in New York City, during the group's East Coast tour! It went on to sell 2.5 million copies in the UK alone, earned the group a gold disc, and coveted the top spot for both Christmas and the New Year, spanning five weeks. Yes, "Merry Xmas Everybody" rounded off Slade's most successful year on the UK charts and was their final chart-topping single.

Slade, who all hailed from the West Midlands, were 'also-rans' of the 1960s, when they embraced the imagery of the skinhead movement. The group comprised drummer Don Powell (born on 10 September 1946 in Bilston) and guitarist Dave Hill (born on 4 April 1946 in Fleet Castle) from The Vendors, a group that gained popularity playing in their local clubs. Guitarist and lead vocalist Neville "Noddy" Holder (born on 15 June 1946 in Walsall) from Steve Brett and the Mavericks, and guitarist Jim Lea (born on 14 June 1949 in Wolverhampton) who cut his musical teeth with the Staffordshire Youth Orchestra. Known as The 'N' Betweens, they recorded poor selling singles for Highland Records and EMI Records, and continued to play the club circuit when they chanced to be seen by Jack Baverstock, head of A&R for Phillips Records.

He signed them to Fontana, changed their name to Ambrose Slade (inspired by a handbag and a pair of shoes) to record their first album "Beginnings" in 1969. Enter their new manager Chas Chandler, former bassist with The Animals, and later manager of Jimi Hendrix. He arranged a recording deal with Polydor Records and persuaded them to ditch the Ambrose tag, change musical style from Stones-esque R&B to raucous rock and roll - and to launch a gimmick for which they'd be remembered: mispelled song titles! The relationship worked. Slade instantly hit with 1971's release "Get Down And Get With It", covering an obscure Little Richard number which rewarded them with a summertime UK top twenty hit.

Buoyed by this success, the group felt it was right to record one of their own songs, to break away from their skinhead image and instead to embrace the flamboyant glam rock movement. All future songs were penned by Noddy

Holder and Jimmy Lea, and with Noddy's powerful, roaring, gritty vocals dominating their material, the cast was set for a string of hit material.

"Coz I Luv You" became Slade's first of six UK number one singles in late 1971, and unlike their previous single it was in a less aggressive and more adult orientated musical style, as was the follow up "Look Wot You Dun", a Top five hit, three months later. The 1972 chart topping singles "Take Me Bak 'Ome" and "Mama Weer All Crazee Now", best typified the group's sound - raw, booty and upbeat; stomping commercial music highlighted by bluesy guitar riffs and Noddy Holder's throaty white R&B vocals. The following year was not only one of glam rock's peak years, but also Slade's strongest on the UK charts. They topped the album chart twice ("Sladest" and "Old, New, Borrowed And Blue"), and scored four hit singles ("Gudbuy T' Jane", "Cum On Feel The Noize" and "Sqweeze Me Pleeze Me") making them the first act to have consecutive releases enter the chart at number one. The last two titles topped the chart, followed by "My Friend Stan" which stalled at number two, and their 1973 Christmas chart topper.

Slade dominated the UK charts during the early 1970s. With their loud music matched only by their stage clothes, particularly those worn by Dave Hill with his short-fringed shoulder length hair, stacked boots and glitter wherever it would stick! However, with success came near tragedy, when Don Powell was involved in a car accident in Wolverhampton during June 1973. He suffered broken ankles and ribs and was left in a coma. His girlfriend was fatally wounded. Slade refused to perform without him. After surgery, Don rejoined the group within ten weeks.

"Merry Xmas Everybody" has since re-charted, in its original form and with The Reading Choir (in 1980), and a dance remix credited to Slade Versus Flush (in 1998) and, of course, regularly appears on Christmas-themed compilation albums.

As fast as Slade had risen so they tumbled. The Christmas single was their final chart topper, although they did come close with "Far Far Away" in late 1974. That proved to be their pentultimate top ten hit of the 1970s – in fact, the glitter on the glam rock was fading as quickly as it had surfaced and followers of the movement were waiting for something new. However, it wasn't the last of Slade. They made an unexpected comeback in the early 1980s; initially signed to Cheapskate Records they recorded 1981's top ten hit , the raucous "We'll Bring The House Down". They then moved to RCA Records, and scored a second string of hits, including a number two hit with the melodic "My Oh My" and a belated US top twenty hit with the anthemic 'Run Run Away'. Returning to Polydor in 1991, the band scored their final hit with "Radio Wall Of Sound", a surprise but welcome comeback, that narrowly missed the UK top twenty, but became a major continental hit.

Twenty years and six number one singles to their credit, Slade in this line-up was over. Noddy retired from the band in the mid 1990s to become a radio/television presenter and an actor. He was awarded the MBE in the 2000 New Year Honours List. His song writing partner Jim Lea went into record production, while Don Powell and Dave Hill continued to perform under the

Slade II name. Just in time for the Christmas market, and backed by a Grange Hill parodying advertising campaign, "The Very Best Of Slade" returned them to the UK album chart in 2005.

Slade can be proud of the fact that they are not only the best selling British-born singles act of the 1970s, but also the most successful group to emerge from the glam rock era, to score hits in two decades with their original membership.

In 2023 it was announced that Noddy Holder was in remission from cancer, diagnosed five years earlier.

UK CHRISTMAS NUMBER ONES 1952-2022

1974

LONELY THIS CHRISTMAS/ I CAN'T STAND IT
MUD

Christmas this year was awash with themed singles including efforts by George Harrison ("Ding Dong"), Wombles ("Wombling Merry Christmas") Gilbert O' Sullivan ("The Christmas Song") and Showaddywaddy ("Hey, Mr Christmas"). But leading the way was a quartet of musical charmers who got lucky after years of commercial failure. And it's all thanks to the power of the stacked glitter heel!

"Lonely This Christmas" rounded off Mud's greatest ever chart year of 1974, when they snatched the mantle of 'Glam Rock Kings' away from Midlands based rivals Slade and Wizzard, as well as from fellow Chinnichap stablemates Sweet, who had, more or less dominated the glam rock scene for the previous two years. Yes, it was time for a change.

While Slade relied on mispelt gimmicks, Wizzard on pantomime, and Sweet on flamboyancy, the visually and musically revamped Mud was inspired by the music and image of the 1950s/1960s. Formed by vocalist Les Gray (born on 9 April 1946), the group's membership was: guitarist/vocalist Dave Mount (born 3 March 1947), bass guitar/vocalist Ray Stiles (born 20 November 1946) and guitar/vocalist Rob Davies (born 1 October 1947) all in Carshalton, Surrey. Like most groups, Mud struggled for recognition, having been associated with record companies, like CBS, Pye and Phillips during the late 1960s, playing music in a similar vein to that made successful by The Move and Pink Floyd.

That lucky break came along with record label owner Mickie Most, who signed them to record for RAK, where Nicky Chinn and Mike Chapman (Chinnichap) were his top writers and producers. Switching musically to the then current glam/glitter rock trend, they were paired up with Chinnichap, who were already successful with other glam acts like American songstress Suzi Quatro, and of course Sweet. Under their RAK Records contract, the group scored instant hits with 1973 hits "Crazy" and "Hypnosis" - both UK top twenty hits. They closed the year with "Dyna-mite", a song originally intended for Sweet but which they rejected. The single exploded into the top five - perhaps its resemblance to Sweet helped, but who knows. It slung Mud flying in the right direction.

The football terrace chant style of "Tiger Feet" dominated the UK top spot for a month in early 1974, while that single's clone "The Cat Crept In" narrowly missed the UK summit in the April. Four months on, "Rocket" peaked inside the top ten, at number six, a lower position than their last two releases. Chinnichap needed a re-think to ensure the group's next release returned them to the top and a Christmas single was the answer! Inspired by the success of Wizzard and Slade the previous Christmas, Nicky and Mike decided to write/produce a seasonal Elvis-sounding rock and roll ballad titled "Lonely This Christmas", with Les Gray doing his greatest Presley vocal impression. It worked. The single was Mud's second of three number one hits of the 1970s, spending a month at the top, sandwiched between the silky and seductive soul/disco of Barry White and the boogie guitar rock of Status Quo. The melodic "The Secrets That You Keep" followed early in 1975, followed by their final chart topper in the April: a lightweight revival of "Oh Boy"; it was also the first of three final UK chart hits for RAK Records – the other two being "Moonshine Sally" reaching the top ten whilst "One Night" the final charting RAK title reaching the top forty during August 1975.

Mud, who by this time, were creating a bit of a frenzy among record companies waiting in the wings for their RAK contract to expire, went on to become the first British act to be signed to the American independent label, Private Stock. While there, they had a positive start with "L-L-Lucy" and "Show Me You're A Woman", both titles were UK top ten entrants. A brief disco/soul musical excursion in 1976's "Shake It Down", and a cover version of Bill Withers's "Lean On Me", both top selling singles, were the last significant titles to chart. Despite a label switch to RCA Records, the end was nigh as the hits quickly dried up. Les Gray signed a solo deal with Warner Bros Records where his take on "A Groovy Kind Of Love" was a top forty entry in early 1977. He then continued to front Mud on the cabaret circuit until his death from a heart attack in February 2004.

The only other member to achieve brief success was Rob Davis who also recorded with rock and roll revivalists, Darts. He later crossed paths with respected dance music DJ/producer, Paul Oakenfold, who in turn inspired Davis to become a best selling dance/pop producer of the new millennium. He co-wrote two UK number one hits: Spiller's "Groovejet (If This Ain't Love)" and Kylie Minogue's "Can't Get You Out Of My Head", in 2000 and 2001 respectively.

Although Mud only dominated the UK chart for three years, they are one of the country's best selling acts of the 20th Century.

Dave Mount died at St Helier's Hospital, Carshalton in December 2006.

UK CHRISTMAS NUMBER ONES 1952-2022

1975

BOHEMIAN RHAPSODY/ I'M IN LOVE WITH MY CAR
QUEEN

The UK chart toppers this year were the most diverse to say the least. They included singing actors, a pair of sixties re-issues, rock 'n'roll remakes, pop pin-ups, soft reggae-pop and Philadelphian soul groups. Then to close the year at the top was a future rock classic courtesy of a rising super group. Generally speaking, record companies are not at ease by extracting an album track for single release without the album being sold to capacity. But radio airplay created public demand for one track, so the company conceded.

Queen, a flamboyant 'pomp-rock' quartet which evolved from Smile, consisted of operatic style vocalist Freddie Mercury (born Frederick Bulsara on 5 September 1946 in Zanzibar, Tanzania: died 24 November 1991), corkscrew haired guitar hero Brian May (born 19 July 1947 in Twickenham, Surrey), ex-teacher turned bassist John Deacon (born 19 August 1951 in Leicester) and photo/videogenic drummer Roger Taylor (born Roger Meddows-Taylor on 26 July 1949 in King's Lynn, Norfolk).

The group's first professional performance was during 1971 at London's Hornsey Town Hall, followed by a string of college and club gigs, and their first UK tour. A year later, they were asked to test new recording equipment at the De Lane Lea Studios, owned by Trident Audio Productions, in return for free recording time. Working with Roy Thomas Baker and John Anthony, engineer/producers of note, Queen recorded several demo tracks. These tracks culminated in a contract with Trident covering production, publishing and management.

EMI Records signed the group to a worldwide deal with the exception of the US where they were represented by WEA/Warners' subsidiary, Elektra. Highlighted by Mercury's strong voice, stage presence and androgynous visual style, Queen scored their first hit with their second single, the March 1974 issued "Seven Seas Of Rhye". (Their debut single was "Keep Yourself Alive") It was thought that the absence of a promotional video for another artist led to them debuting on Top Of The Pops, the BBC's premier music programme, which in turn elevated "Seven Seas Of Rhye" into the top ten, from their debut self-titled album. Their second, "Queen II", hit the top five, although it was classed as one of their lesser known releases with its white side and black side.

UK CHRISTMAS NUMBER ONES 1952-2022

After hitting number two in late 1974 with their third album "Sheer Heart Attack", and the "Killer Queen" single, it took another year before Queen were to score the much wanted pole position on both singles and albums charts. Having undertaken promotional tours across the world, including a successful Japanese trek, the group spent the bulk of 1975 recording their next album "A Night At The Opera" and its lead single – "Bohemian Rhapsody". The track ran for five minutes and 55 seconds - too long for single release. However, nobody reckoned on Kenny Everett.

The zany radio DJ, who was a friend of Freddie Mercury's, constantly played the track in full on his Capital Radio show. Calls swamped the station's switchboard and public demand heightened until EMI Records had no choice but to release the track as a single in its entirety and likely perhaps through the gritted teeth of the EMI shirts and ties! The song was recorded in sections – ballad, guitar solo with operatic and hard rock sequences. The most expensive single ever recorded (at the time) as well as being the most elaborate in styling. The demand for "Bohemian Rhapsody" was such that it dominated the UK singles chart for nine long weeks, selling one million copies in a month, and later becoming the UK's third best selling single of all time. The promotional video was groundbreaking, and set an extremely high standard to follow. A rock masterpiece!

Its appeal was universal and was the obvious candidate for the Christmas top spot of 1975 as, unlike the two previous years of the mid 1970s, there wasn't a rash of Christmas songs to compete with. The only notable festive fare eager for that all important Christmas number one was Dana's 'It's Gonna Be A Cold Cold Christmas' a respectable top five hit, and Greg Lake's equally impressive 'I Believe in Father Christmas' which reached number two. While previous Christmas number ones of the decade to date were of a jovial nature, Bohemian Rhapsody may have seemed tongue in cheek but it was a rock masterpiece waiting to happen. When it did, it became their best selling single. Although not the first ever promo, the songs visual companion was no frills and broke the rule of the rock promo video, it showed more than the band performing and performing it had a concept.

"Bohemian Rhapsody" went on to win the Ivor Novello award for Best Selling British Single Of 1975, while "A Night At The Opera" peaked in the UK top ten. The album's packaging featured the re-worked Queen crest (included on their previous two albums) featuring the group members' birth signs - two Leo lions (Deacon and Taylor) two Virgo fairies (Mercury) and one Cancer crab for May. The album topped the UK chart, passed platinum sales and spawned the further single "You're My Best Friend".

"Bohemian Rhapsody" has since been recorded by numerous and diverse acts, like the UK comedy rock outfit Bad News in 1987, and American female duo The Braids during 1996. It tied with Procol Harum's "A Whiter Shade Of Pale" as Best British Pop Single 1952-1977 at the BRITS ceremony to celebrate the Queen Elizabeth's Silver Jubilee year (1977). And Queen would take the single to the top of the UK chart once more. Of the many awards the song won over the years, one of the most prestigious was being inducted into the Grammy Hall of Fame during 2004.

(See also Christmas 1991)

1976

WHEN A CHILD IS BORN (SOLEADO)/ EVERYTIME YOU TOUCH ME (I GET HIGH)
JOHNNY MATHIS

An American icon, a housewives' favourite, a former athlete, a successful album seller, and one of the first openly gay superstar singers. These are the many ways that can best describe the man who was born in Gilmer, Texas, on 30 September 1935, one of seven children who, with their parents moved to San Francisco where he grew up - and who dominated this year's Christmas chart.

He was born into a musical family and studied opera as a teenager. He also excelled in athletics, planning to be a physical education teacher when he left school. However, his love of music overpowered him as he signed a recording contract with Columbia Records in 1955. He was influenced by singers like Billy Eckstine, Nat King Cole and Ella Fitzgerald but attempts to establish himself in the jazz market failed, so his record company assigned him to Mitch Miller, who had other ideas. The relationship worked and a series of husky-voiced ballads attracted the public. In 1956 "Wonderful! Wonderful!" established him in the middle of the road market to become a huge US hit, selling one million copies."It's Not For Me To Say" and the double headed "Chances Are"/"Twelfth Of Never" followed a year later. The latter title hit the US top four. Both were two million sellers each

His UK career began in 1958 when "Teacher Teacher" was released on the Fontana label to peak in the top thirty, followed by two further titles which reached the top five and twenty respectively – "A Certain Smile" and "Winter Wonderland". In 1959 he scored two UK hits with "Someone" and "The Best Of Everything", while his popularity in the US went from strength to strength with top selling titles like "Come To Me", "Misty" and "Gina". By now he had also released several big grossing albums including "Johnny Mathis' Greatest Hits", which stayed around the UK chart for ten years.

Remarkably, by 1963 his career was showing signs of deteriorating. He left Columbia Records to sign with Mercury Records. His last US top ten single "What Will Mary Say" hit the top fifty in the UK, while his final US hit "Life Is A Song Worth Singing" died in the top sixty in 1964. As the Mercury connection had not worked, Johnny Mathis returned to Columbia Records in an attempt to pick up the pieces of his career.

When the 1970s dawned, he had embraced a more soulful R&B sound, obviously influenced by the successful Philly Soul as evident with songs such as a version of The Stylistics' "I'm Stone In Love With You" - a number one UK hit in 1975. His long standing relationship with Columbia Records (now owned by Sony/BMG Entertainment) perhaps encouraged his confidence to embrace other genres of popular music. His return to middle of the road material resulted in his only (to date) British number one single which is inoffensive but, however, comes across as slightly 'twee'.

"When A Child Is Born", previously European hits for Italian singer Ciro Dammico, and the German native Michael Holm, before it was re-recorded by Johnny Mathis. It wasn't intended to be a Christmas song but its lyrical content, hymnal harmonies and lush orchestration held the perfect ingredients for that all important Christmas number one spot, knocking Showaddywaddy's rendition of "Under The Moon Of Love" off the pole position at the last minute. Johnny's single went on to sell six million copies worldwide.

Johnny Mathis, or rather "When A Child Is Born", triggered a brief middle of the road music revolt in early 1977, as the first eight UK number one singles of that year were of a lightweight nature. When he tried to repeat the magic of the Christmas chart topper in 1981 by duetting with soul singer Gladys Knight, it failed miserably. Unfortunately, Johnny was unable to hold on to his selling power and his career hit the decline button once again.

That is until 1978 when he duetted with the sweet voiced soul/gospel artist Deniece Williams on "Too Much Too Little Too Late" - a number three UK hit and US chart topper. It sold five million copies. An album together followed, from which the second duet was lifted titled "You're All I Need To Get By". Their version of the Marvin Gaye and Tammi Terrell classic peaked in the UK and US top fifty.

In 1980, and following his solo UK hit "Gone Gone Gone", Johnny Mathis recorded "Different Kinda Different" with Paulette Williams. Two years later, he recorded "Friends In Love" with Dionne Warwick, and in 1984 returned to Deniece Williams to sing "Love Won't Let Me Wait". Mathis continued to sell albums, and has made a serious living - like most artists of his stature – performing at concerts and the predictable Vegas style jaunts. In between times, Johnny published his cook book Cooking For You Alone.

It was rumoured that in the late 1980s, British super producers and writers StockAitken/Waterman came close - but not close enough - to write and produce for Johnny Mathis, because Columbia was impressed with their success on the US chart. It also appeared that Pete Waterman admired the voice behind the Christmas number one single in 1976.

During his life Johnny Mathis has undergone treatment for alcohol abuse and prescribed drug addiction. He supports various charities including The Muscular Dystrophy Association and the American Cancer Society.

UK CHRISTMAS NUMBER ONES 1952-2022

In 2011 – and with a reported 350 million records sold – Johnny Mathis released a new album for Sony Records titled "Let It Be Me" which was critically applauded and two years later issued the seasonal "Sending You A Little Christmas" album, with his most recent studio release "Johnny Mathis Sings The Great New American Songbook".

His next comeback is avidly awaited.

1977

MULL OF KINTYRE/ GIRLS SCHOOL
WINGS

With its country/folk style guitar intro and almost waltz time melody, the lead of this double-headed single was far removed from anything that Paul McCartney did before and anything since. It was the only single to hit the top spot under the Wings group, so named by McCartney following a flash of inspiration while waiting in London's King College Hospital for his daughter Mary to be born.

"Mull Of Kintyre", written by Paul McCartney and former Moody Blues singer Denny Laine, was inspired by the landscape of the Scottish peninsula close Campbeltown Farm - where the McCartney family lived. The song's melodic easy listening style, far removed from the group's previous mainstream rock style, was accompanied by 21 members of the local bagpipe and drum band, and topped the chart for nine weeks, with sales past two million, becoming the biggest selling UK single of all time until Band Aid's "Do They Know It's Christmas?" in 1984. "Mull of Kintyre" won a host of awards including the Best Selling A-Side category at the 23rd annual Ivor Novello Awards in 1978. In the US, the single was flipped for release because Wings' record company Capitol believed the UK topside lacked confidence and would not attract the record buyers. "Girls School" hit the US mainstream top forty, while MOR radio stations favoured "Mull Of Kintyre", which pushed it into the top 45 on the Adult Contemporary singles chart.

When The Beatles completed "Let It Be", their last album as a group, Paul McCartney had already finished his debut solo album. The group had been dogged with disagreements until the situation was untenable. The growing rifts bounced from one group member to the other, so the only way out was to disolve, which they did in 1970. Legal action followed until the group's finances were settled in a way agreeable to each member.

The mellifluous "Another Day", extracted from McCartney's first self-named album, hit number two in the UK, equalling the peak of the parent album. A year later he released "Ram" which included his wife, Linda Eastman's name. They first met at the London club, Bag O'Nails and married in 1969. Her inclusion into the group was not, at first, welcomed by fans. In 1972, McCartney officially announced the line-up of Wings, namely, ex Moody Blues member Denny Laine (born 29 October 1944 in Birmingham), Denny Seiwell (born 10 July 1943), The Grease Band's Henry McCullough (born 21 June 1943 in Portstewart, Northern Ireland), Linda (born 24 September 1941, New York City, New York) and himself. As such, they issued "Back Seat Of My Car", a top forty UK hit, while "Uncle Albert" hit the US pole position.

After the release of the group's second album "Wings Wildlife", they undertook their first UK tour, taking in dates on the college circuit. Horrified at the carnage from the Bloody Sunday Massacre in Northern Ireland, McCartney wrote the strong worded "Give Ireland Back To The Irish". The single was instantly banned by BBC Radio 1, prompting Wings to release "Mary Had A Little Lamb" - a nursery rhyme set to music – as their next single. Nobody could be offended by that! It was a UK top ten hit in June 1972. Once again, McCartney's music was banned. This time with his next single "Hi Hi Hi" reputedly drugs related, and this was very much in the public eye, as Paul and Linda had been arrested twice during the year for possession of cannabis.

In 1973 Wings released the "Red Rose Speedway" album, and a year later their finest work to date "Band On The Run", which went on to sell over six million copies universally, topping the world's charts. "My Love" was one of the high calibre tracks to be lifted as a single.

A musical contrast followed when McCartney wrote the theme for the forthcoming James Bond film "Live And Let Die". Full of thunder and in the distinctive Bond styling, performed by Brenda Arnau on the actual film soundtrack. "Helen Wheels", "Jet", "Band On The Run" ensured Wing's high chart profile through to 1975.

During 1974 Geoff Britton joined Wings, and a year later was replaced by Joe English, when the "Venus And Mars" album was issued, from which "Listen To What The Man Said" was extracted as a single. The album hit the top spot, the single peaked in the top ten. At this time, the group embarked upon a long-overdue UK tour which spread across ten countries, into America. "Letting Go", "Silly Love Songs" and "Let 'Em In" were released while they were on the road. All big sellers. Also during 1977, Joe English and Henry McCulloch left the group.

Selecting a follow-up to "Mull Of Kintyre" was impossible, so a chirpy "With A Little Luck" hit the streets and shelves, with not a bagpipe to be heard! Selling over 2.5 million copies, the single hit the UK top five and the US top spot. The ex-Beatle's sixth single to reach that position. Reduced to a trio, McCartney continued his regular chart run with singles including "I've Had Enough", "Goodnight Tonight" and "Old Siam Sir"; plus the albums "London Town", "Wings Greatest" and "Back To The Egg".

Now the proud recipient of a rhodium medallion, presented during a "Guinness Book Of Records" ceremony, in recognition of his song writing career that included 43 songs from 1962 to 1978, Paul McCartney was recognised as the most successful composer of all time. It was as a soloist that he continued in the music business because in early 1980 he laid Wings to rest. It seems unlikely that the name will be revived because it was associated with Denny Laine and Linda McCartney who died from breast cancer during 1998. She was 56 years old.

Paul McCartney recruited a hand-picked selection of musicians to support him in the recording studio and on tour, so perhaps the group element isn't totally lost. Wings might be defunct but its founder and leader – Sir James Paul McCartney MBE - continues to take huge musical strides, and to this year (2023) he is as much in the public eye as he ever was. A true British icon and national treasure!

(See also Christmas 1963, 1964, 1965 and 1967)

UK CHRISTMAS NUMBER ONES 1952-2022

1978

MARY'S BOY CHILD/ OH MY LORD
BONEY M

Recap the UK singles/albums charts of the late 1970s, and it's synonymous with not just disco, punk, groundbreaking film soundtracks and its spin-off hit singles or endless Elvis re-issues, but artists strongly associated with that era, such as the Eagles, Chic, Blondie, David Soul and, of course, Abba. Plus the unique outfit who was the top selling singles act of 1978. It may come as a surprise to learn that Abba never scored a UK number one Christmas single, although their albums would be high on music lovers' present lists.

Named after an Australian police drama series Boney, with the 'M' evolving from the female members' name initial, the group was formed in Germany by producer Frank Farian. He had in fact recorded "Baby Do You Wanna Bump" under the name Boney M, and when the single took off he needed a 'group' to perform it. So, he hired Maizie Williams, Sheyla Bonnick and a male dancer, with a third female singer later hired only to be replaced later on by Claudja Barry. She left in 1976 to pursue a successful career as a disco artist. Eventually, the line-up settled down and with Maizie Williams (born on 25 March 1951 in Montserrat, West Indies), were Marcia Bennett (born on 14 October 1948 in St Catherines, Jamaica) Liz Mitchell (born on 12 July 1952 in Clarenden, Jamaica) and Bobby Farrell (born on 6 October 1949 in Aruba, West Indies). Boney M's first album "Take The Heat Off Me" in 1976 was followed by their first UK charting title "Daddy Cool" late in the year, and their version of Bobby Hebb's "Sunny", both top ten entrants. Their second album "Love For Sale" contained more hits – and the fun continued.

Signed to the European label, Hansa, their UK releases appeared on Atlantic/WEA Records (with both Hansa and Atlantic logo's sharing joint label credit on releases). They scored four top ten UK singles in 1977 – "Daddy Cool" and "Sunny", followed by "Ma Baker" which peaked at number two, and "Belfast", a top ten hit. Although 1977 was a good year for the band, the next year saw them peaking career-wise, and earning the title of the best selling singles act on the UK chart.

Their "Night Flight To Venus" album housed the chart topper "Rivers Of Babylon"/"Brown Girl In The Ring" which went on to sell a staggering two million copies, and the UK number two hit "Rasputin". It also held an adaptation of a West Indian carol "Mary's Boy Child" which would give Boney

M their second UK chart topper. Best known via Harry Belafonte's million seller from twenty one years' previous (also a UK Christmas number one which also sold in excess of two million copies – see Christmas 1957), Boney M's rendition was combined with Farian's own composition "Oh My Lord", recorded in the band's adopted calypso, pop/funk style, which enabled Bobby Farrell to dance in whatever style the mood took him. They dominated the singles chart throughout December, and it's plain to see why. The single was in the style of a traditional Christmas song and was unlike many Festive themed songs of that decade.

Incorporating Frank Farian's composition provided a financial safeguard for him whenever sales and airplay rotation totals were tallied. Talking of totals and tallies, Warner Brothers' British office must have rubbed their hands in delight during this period, because Boney M's single and album sales easily recouped (and more) the allocated promotional budgets!

Boney M were at their professional peak, so frenetic demands were made on them for them to be seen anywhere and everywhere, while their record company started footing the bill for the safe overseas transportation to Germany of their numerous silver, gold and platinum discs, representing escalating sales of their product!

The follow up to "Night Flight To Venus" was "Oceans Of Fantasy" in September 1979, their second number one album. Once again the release contained top ten hits with "Painter Man" and "Hooray Hooray, It's A Holi-Holiday", but, sadly, their last, because it seemed that the once faithful British audience, who instantly took the Munich-based foursome to their hearts, was just as quickly finding them rather tiresome.

Boney M were destined to be consigned as '1970s stars', because by the start of the next decade they struggled for hits with singles including "My Friend Jack" and "Children Of Paradise". However, the group didn't disappear entirely, it re-charted in 1992 with a "Boney M Megamix" which reached the UK top ten, while a remix of "Brown Girl In The Ring" struggled into the top forty. However, the Telstar promoted "The Greatest Hits" shot into the top twenty. A 'mash-up' mix of "Ma Baker" with "Somebody Scream" credited to Boney M vs Horny United, reached the top 30 in 1999; two years on a remixed "Daddy Cool" struggled into the top fifty, as did a re-issue of "Mary's Boy Child/Oh My Lord". Each time they enjoyed chart success, it seemed like a serious revival was on the cards for Boney M, but alas that was never to be, and the act instead took that ticket back to revival tours, college campuses, and anywhere their talent was appreciated.

As recently as 2011, they were still certified as one of the best selling overseas singles/albums act in the UK. They never had the same cultural adulation awarded to their contemporaries like Abba, because perhaps, Boney M was a producer/writer medium and were often viewed with sceptic dismissal.

A West End musical Daddy Cool, in which the songs of Boney M formed the basis of its story, became a stage hit. This led their entire recording output being made available once again through the SonyBMG subsidiary Ariola (who currently own the rights to their back catalogue). This resulted in a chart success during 2006 with "The Very Best Of Boney M".

Tragedy closed the classic Boney M line up, when 61 year old Bobby Farrell died from heart failure on 30th December 2010. Even without their entertaining male dancer, the memory of Boney M lives on via the probable endless recycling of greatest hits packages, uploaded performance clips across the internet and soundalike groups.

A revamped Boney M continues to tour the world and, while the line up may have changed, their music lives on for future generations. Rightly or wrongly!

1979

ANOTHER BRICK IN THE WALL (PART II)/ ONE OF MY TURNS
PINK FLOYD

The final number one UK single of the 1970s came from that decade's best selling British album group in the US! However, the achievement wasn't without its problems in the guise of line-up changes and personal demons that plagued them. "Another Brick In The Wall (Part II)" was one of a trilogy of songs that were variations on the same theme featured on their 1979 album "The Wall". It was also Pink Floyd's first UK hit single since 1967 with "See Emily Play".

Roger Waters, born 6 September 1944 in Great Bookham, Surrey, met Nick Mason, born 27th January 1945 in Birmingham, West Midlands, at London's Regent Street Polytechnic. They formed their first group Sigma 6 with Richard Wright, born 28 July 1943 in Hatch End, Middlesex (died 15 September 2008), later becoming The Architectural Abdabs. Prior to the name change, Syd Barrett, born 6 January 1946 in Cambridge (died 7 July 2006), joined the line-up, whereupon they become known as The Pink Floyd Sound, taken from the Carolina businessman Pink Anderson and Floyd Council.

In 1965 the group performed its first professional date at London's Countdown Club, which led to future gigs at the Marquee Club, where their repertoire switched from R&B to Syd Barrett's original compositions, complete with lengthy instrumental breaks, the first indication of the group's interest in psychedelia. Following this outstanding performance, the group signed a six-way management contract with Andrew King and Peter Jenner, naming the company Blackhill Enterprises.

By 1967 Pink Floyd were a growing musical force; they were more fashionable and forward thinking than some of the charting acts of the time despite not having a single released. Eventually, EMI Records secured them for the reputed signing fee of £5,000, one of the highest at the time. "Arnold Layne" – telling the story of a transvestite who stole women's underwear from washing lines - was the group's debut single in March 1967. Due to the risqué nature of the lyrics, the title was immediately banned by the mainstream BBC stations, but thankfully pirate station Caroline plugged it nonstop. With their help "Arnold Layne" hit the UK top twenty. "See Emily Play" followed to hit the top ten, with their first album "The Piper At The Gates Of Dawn" issued in the August. Another top ten hit. Within a month of its release, Pink Floyd embarked upon a US tour, but the trip was cut short when Syd Barrett, who was mentally unstable and now a regular LSD user, was unable to work. The band continued to work with him until the situation became unworkable. Dave Gilmour, born 6 March 1947 in Cambridge, replaced Barrett in 1968, Pete Jenner and Andrew King also moved on, believing the group would suffer without Syd's input as prime composer.

After the release of two poor selling singles – "It Would Be Nice" and "Point Me" – and the top ten album "A Saucerful Of Secrets", Pink Floyd continued to widely perform in high profile concerts, like, the National Jazz, Pop and Blues Festival. A pair of albums were also released: "More", the soundtrack to the movie of the same name, and "Ummagumma", a top five title in 1969. Meanwhile, Syd Barrett signed a solo deal with EMI Records where his single "Octopus" was issued in the December.

Pink Floyd decided to abandon the singles medium to concentrate on recording albums; it was a highly lucrative market, and artistically, was not confining to three or more minutes. "Atom Heart Mother" was a 1970 chart topper, followed by "Relics" a year later from which "Arnold Layne" and "See Emily Play" were extracted.

The group spent their professional life touring and recording, ensuring their name was a regular addition to the album charts. But nothing prepared the listening public for their 1973 album "Dark Side Of The Moon", where their music explored the inner, rather than the outer space, highlighting the emotions attached to lunacy, death and insecurity. It was a masterpiece in the true sense of the word, and spent 300 weeks on its initial UK chart run after peaking at number two.

In the US, the album spent a staggering 741 weeks on the chart, after spending one week at the top. Sales passed the 20 million mark quite easily. Two years later, "Wish You Were Here" crashed both the UK and US album charts at the top, and in 1977 "Animals", a four track album, hit number two in the UK, and a rung lower in the US. In between releases, Pink Floyd continued to tour but this time they were filling 50,000 capacity stadiums across the world. When not working as a group, the individual members worked on solo projects. They next united for "The Wall", conceived by Roger Waters, which spanned two albums to be released in 1979. "Another Brick In The Wall (Part II)" held the UK pole position for five weeks; four weeks in the US, while the album hit the top spot across the world.

Joining the group on the single was the Islington Green School choir, for which they received £1,000 donation. The group took their "Wall" on tour with costly pieces of stage equipment that included 30-feet-high, 160-feet-long brick wall which separated the audience from the performing group. Midway through their act, the wall was destroyed. In July 1982, the film "The Wall", starring Bob Geldof as Pink, a burned-out rock star, and a profusion of Gerald Scarfe animations, premiered in London. And the following year, Pink Floyd issued their third UK chart topping album "The Final Cut" from which Not Now John" was lifted as a top thirty single.

With Rick Wright departed from the line-up, David Gilmour and Roger Waters embarked on solo careers again, but the pull of Pink Floyd was too great to ignore. Despite legal action, Waters could not stop David Gilmour, Rick Wright and Nick Mason using the group name for recording and touring purposes. As such the album "A Momentary Lapse Of Reason" and single "Only Learning To Fly" were released: the album hit the top three in both the UK and US, while the single died. "On The Turning Away" single was issued as the group began a world tour. It peaked in the UK top thirty, while its follow-up "One Slip" stalled in the top forty.

Through the 1990s Pink Floyd continued to tour and record. On 2 July 2005 they reunited for Live 8, the global awareness event staged in London's Hyde Park, organised to coincide with the G8 conference being held in Scotland. By 2013 the group has sold in excess of 250 million records worldwide and are still revered as one of the most influential rock groups of all time, with their psychedelic fused music, hard hitting lyrics and complexly exciting concerts.

Proving also that the Pink Floyd brand still carries weight, David Gilmour released the solo album project "Rattle That Lock" , released by Columbia Records and co-produced with Roxy Music alumni Phil Manzanera , it was a hefty selling item the world over late in 2015.

Following the acquisition/merger/reconstruction of EMI Records within Universal Music and due to EU regulators several notable EMI signings including Pink Floyd, Cliff Richard ,David Bowie and Kate Bush were transferred over to rival company Warner Music as part of the Parlophone divestment sale by Universal to Warner – so let the repackaging and re-releasing begin!

Plus no self respecting golden oldie radio station or retro school disco club would be complete without the classic "Another Brick In The Wall (Part II)". What a proud legacy to share through the generations.

1980

THERE'S NO ONE QUITE LIKE GRANDMA/ PINOCCHIO
ST WINIFRED'S SCHOOL CHOIR

The first Christmas number one of the 1980s didn't come from the New Romantics, established chart veterans or a teen idol of some description, but a school choir from northern England. And nobody saw it coming - least of all the chart compilers!.

Stockport-based St Winifred's Roman Catholic Primary School first tasted chart success when some of its pupils performed on Brian & Michael's "Matchstalk Men And Matchstalk Cats And Dogs", a charttopper in 1978. It was this that inspired Sister Aquinas, the head teacher at the Primary School, to form a choir in the hope of repeating the success. The choir failed to score the previous Christmas with "Bread And Fishes", but hit the jackpot by spending two weeks at the top of the Christmas chart in 1980 with their only hit single "There's No One Quite Like Grandma". Penned by Gordon Lorenz for the HM the Queen Mother's 80th Birthday, his version was rejected by EMI Records' Music For Pleasure label, but when someone suggested to try it with St Winifred's School Choir, who were already signed to the label, the song worked. Their tear-jerking yet thought provoking ode to grandma avoided any labels of 'twee', but rather cries of 'aah', because of the sweet voice of eight year old Dawn Ralph, which appealed to younger family members who were more likely to purchase the record for their elders.

"There's No One Quite Like Grandma" held all those vital ingredients for that all important number one at Christmas time, but the unthinkable murder of John Lennon could easily have given Christmas 1980 a totally different charttopper. Lennon was in the chart with "(Just Like) Starting Over", it had peaked at number eight and had dropped out of the top twenty altogether, when he was gunned down by obsessed fan Mark Chapman. The single reversed track immediately to the top, only to be replaced by St Winifred's School Choir.

Actress Sally Lindsay, who years later starred in the popular BBC television series The Royle Family, and as Shelley Unwin in ITV's long running soap Coronation Street, was among the young voices in St Winifred's School Choir.

Twenty nine years later, in November 2009, 14 members of the Choir, most now grown up with children of their own, reunited to record a new version of their 1980 charttopper to raise funds for Age Concern and Help The Aged.

1981

DON'T YOU WANT ME/ SECONDS
HUMAN LEAGUE

They hailed from the South Yorkshire industrial town of Sheffield, and were one of the most consistent selling New Wave acts of the 1980s. A six-piece outfit, not as some people believed, a trio. The striking visual image of a dark-haired male with a lopsided wedge bob and two teenage girls, one blonde, the other brunette, both sporting 'blitz' hair styles.

The Human League's origin began in 1977 as a Sheffield-based male trio The Future, consisting of lead singer Philip Oakey (born on 2 October 1955), with Martyn Ware (born on 19 May 1956) and Ian Craig Marsh (born on 11 November 1956). In 1978 they renamed themselves Human League – the name swiped from the science fiction game Starforce: Alpha Centauri - and toured as support acts for Siouxsie and the Banshees, and Iggy Pop. These dates led to major label interest, and ultimately a recording contract with Virgin Records in 1979. But a year later, both Martyn Ware and Ian Craig Marsh defected to form Heaven 17, and sold the rights to the Human League name to Oakey in exchange for 1% of any royalties earned under that name.

Phil Oakey subsequently reformed Human League recruiting bassist/synsthesist Ian Burden (born on 24 December 1957), Adrian Wright (born on 30 June 1956), ex-Rezillos guitarist Jo Callis (born on 2 May 1955), and schoolgirls cum cocktail waitresses, Suzanne Sulley (born on 22 March 1963) and Joanne Catherall (born on 18 September 1962) to complete the group's the new look line up.

With that distinctive visual image of the lopsided fringed Phil Oakey and his the two teenage singers, the group soon became chart regulars with 1981 being their greatest year, scoring five UK singles including "Sound Of The Crowd" (number two), "Love Action (I Believe In)" (credited as Human League Red) (number three), and the song which was to be the Christmas number one – "Don't You Want Me". (A year earlier, "Holiday 80 (Double Single)" was their first charting item, followed by "Empire State Human", both top sixty hits.)

Like their chart singles to date, "Don't You Want Me" was produced by the Strangler's Martin Rushent, and written by Callis/Wright/Oakey, in their trademarked synthesised style, with a more pronounced commercial slant, causing arguments within the group that they had lost their original sound. The band's fear of selling out was unfounded, as the single gave both them and Virgin Records their first ever UK number one single, dominating the top spot for five weeks. Its success was helped by its 'film-within-a-film' concept promotional video. It also opened the floodgates for a global breakthrough, aided as well by the success of the single's parent album "Dare" which topped the album chart two months earlier. "Don't You Want Me" also topped the US Hot 100 the following summer, with "Dare" reaching the top five, cementing the fact that Human League were strongly part of the second 'Brit Invasion' of the early 1980s.

As a token of their appreciation Phil Oakey was given a BMW motorbike by Virgin Records. Most certainly at this time it seemed that Human League were the true New Romantic darlings.

After a successful run of hits over the next three years, that included the re-issue from 1978, "Being Boiled", "Mirror Man" and "(Keep Feeling) Fascination" – both top two hits in 1982 and 1983, and "Life On Your Own", "Louise" in 1984. An unlikely, yet rewarding, collaboration with the US R&B writing/production duo Jimmy Jam and Terry Lewis, returned them to the top of the US chart a second time in 1986 with "Human". It was also a UK top ten hit, followed by "I Need Your Loving", "Love Is All That Matters" and "Heart Like A Wheel" saw them through to the 1990s.

Switching labels to a Warners' subsidiary East West, (Atlantic in America) secured their final UK top ten single (to date) with 1995's "Tell Me When". Other singles followed like "One Man In My Heart", "Filling Up With Heaven" and "Stay With Me Tonight" – all mid-selling offerings. Five years later the act surfaced on the Chrysalis Group's Papillion logo to release the album "Secret" and score a reasonable dance hit with "All I Ever Wanted" , with their previous company, Virgin, planning a remix campaign to cash in on the group's brief chart comeback. Only a dance remix of "Don't You Want Me" was issued to chart inside the top twenty. In 2003, "Love Me Madly" also from "Secrets" was issued. Then, two years later, EMI Records released "The Human League – Original Remixes And Rarities" compilation, and to mark the group's 30th anniversary in the music business they toured across twenty European dates including London.

In 2011 Human League, with line-up changes, issued the studio album "Credo" on Wall Of Sound Records. Although it never quite reached those commercial peaks of the 1980s. A year on they toured Europe and the UK again to celebrate their 35th anniversary this time.

As for "Don't You Want Me", the song shows no danger of fading, it re-entered the chart (in it's original mix) yet again in early 2014 due to an intense social media campaign by fans of Aberdeen Football Club; numerous cover versions - including a parody of the lyrics/melody for a UK car advertising campaign – have proven the song's resilience that is as strong as the fashion conscious band who first wrote and performed it.

UK CHRISTMAS NUMBER ONES 1952-2022

1982

SAVE YOUR LOVE/ LOVE IS NOT THE REASON
RENEE & RENATO

1982 may well be remembered as this decade's year where the corniest of records topped the chart. It had for example, classic singles by The Jam ("Town Called Malice") Dexy's Midnight Runners ("Come On Eileen") and Musical Youth ("Pass The Dutchie"); as well as successful re-issues by Irene Cara ("Fame") and Charlene ("I've Never Been To Me") alongside unlikely bedfellows like Captain Sensible ("Happy Talk") Tight Fit ("The Lion Sleeps Tonight"), and "Ebony And Ivory", the duet from Paul McCartney and Stevie Wonder - and this Christmas number one single!

Italian born in June 1940, Birmingham restaurant owner Renato Pagliari, and English singer Hilary Lester, recorded "Save Your Love", written by a husband and wife, John and Sue Edward specifically for them. (John was behind another 1980s pop culture icon, the robot Metal Mickey.) The single was released on the Edward's independent label Hollywood and was its second release and first chart topper for the indie distributor Pinnacle.

Renato had auditioned for ITV's top talent show New Faces during 1975. He was spotted there by John Edward, who teamed him with Hilary Lester, renaming them Renee and Renato. By the time the single was issued, Renee had left the partnership to team up with another band. She later returned to her previous lifestyle.

"Save Your Love" was an operatic love ballad, performed with Italian panache which probably fooled record buyers. It was accompanied by a promotional video featuring Renato with his singing partner replaced by actress Val Penney, whose face was, by necessity, obscured throughout. Two further singles that included the returning Renee, followed – "Just One Kiss", a top fifty hit in 1983, and "Jesus Loves Us All" which flopped.

Rightly or wrongly, "Save Your Love" has since been considered to be one of the worst UK number one singles of the decade, yet Renato continued to perform and guest spot on television entertainment shows like Little And Large. Renato died at the age of 69 at the Good Hope Hospital, Sutton Coldfield, in July 2009, leaving a unique and typically quirky legacy. He was the vocalist on the Wall's ice cream jingle "Just One Cornetto", and being one half responsible for a song voted as one of the 50 Greatest One Hit Wonders in a 2006 television poll.

UK CHRISTMAS NUMBER ONES 1952-2022

1983

ONLY YOU/DISCO DOWN
THE FLYING PICKETS

Six actors/vocalists naming themselves after a term used to describe travelling strikers to record a song that was almost two years old, but performed in a style, dramatically altered from its original version, secured the top spot this year.

Brainchild of Brian Hibbard, the group was groomed in the socialist theatre company known as John McGrath's 7:84. The distinctive acapella vocal outfit performed in the 1981 play One Big Blow telling the story of the miner's strike, and as some of the group members had actually been active in the strikes during the early 1970s, they chose the name The Flying Pickets. Joining Brian Hibbard in the original line up were Rick Lloyd, Ken Gregson, Gareth Williams, David Brett and Red Stripe (David Gittins). Four of the membership wore loud suits and unsuitable hats, while Hibbard sported oversized sideburns, and Stripe favoured eye liner. And together they recorded a stripped down accapella version of Yazoo's "Only You", penned by Vince Clarke, while a member of Depeche Mode.

Released by 10 Records, a subsidiary of Virgin Records, their harmonic version was perfect for the Christmas season. It dominated the top of the UK chart for a month, along the way giving birth to foreign language versions, and the offer of supporting American superstar, Dionne Warwick on a number of tour dates. Not only that, but The Flying Pickets gave the UK its first ever acapella number one single.

Their next two singles were also cover versions. The first was written for Ruby and the Romantics titled "When You're Young And In Love" (a number seven hit), while the second was the Eurythmics' "Who's That Girl" (number 71). The group musically peaked in 1984 which coincided with the miners strike, and when they publicly supported it, their record company was not amused. It was perhaps the group's political views that influenced their selling power. In their live shows, The Flying Pickets selected a wide range of repertoire ranging from Bob Marley, Talking Heads, Smokey Robinson and The Red Hot Chilli Peppers, to perform in their unique acapella style, but this was not enough to sustain them as a chart act. Instead, the group continued to perform with varied line-up changes, but never charted again.

In the mid-1980s, Brian Hibbard and Red Stripe left the group to release a poor selling version of Yazoo's "Mr Blue". Hibbard returned to acting to appear in the television peak viewing programmes Coronation Street, Dr

Who and Doctors. He also starred in the 1997 film Twin Town, and won a BAFTA for his role in Little White Lies. On the other hand, Red Stripe moved to Australia.

In 2010, a totally revamped Flying Pickets travelled to America to record the Christmas-themed, 12 tracked "Only Yule" album, later available via i-Tunes, which included a remake of "Only You" – naturally!

Brian Hibbard died at the age of 65 in June 2012, after a long battle with cancer.

1984

DO THEY KNOW IT'S CHRISTMAS?/ FEED THE WORLD
BAND AID

During October 1984 a BBC TV news item showed Michael Buerk reporting on the plight of the famine which had hit the people of Ethiopia. The dreadful scenes moved Bob Geldof so much that he decided to raise funds to help feed this starving population. He contacted Midge Ure from Ultravox and together they composed "Do They Know It's Christmas?" which went on to become the biggest selling single in UK chart history, selling one million copies within the first week of its release. (Elton John's version of "Candle In The Wind" which was re-written following the death of Diana, Princess of Wales in 1997 replaced it as the top selling single).

Once the song was completed, Bob Geldof contacted the Sarm West Studios, London. Its owner Trevor Horn donated 24 hours free recording time. Next, the best of UK acts were contacted and they arrived en masse to offer their services free at the recording studio on 25 November.

The final line-up read: U2's Bono and Adam Clayton, Phil Collins, The Boomtown Rats' Bob Geldof, Simon Crowe, Pete Briquette and Johnny Fingers, Spandau Ballet's Steve Norman, Tony Hadley, Martin Kemp, John Keeble and Gary Kemp, Ultravox's Chris Cross and Midge Ure, Duran Duran's John Taylor, Simon Le Bon, Roger Taylor, Andy Taylor and Nick Rhodes, Paul Young, Heaven 17's Glenn Gregory and Martin Ware, Marilyn, Bananarama's Keren, Sara and Siobhan, Shalamar's Jody Watley, Paul Weller, Kool and the Gang's James Taylor, Robert 'Kool' Bell and Dennis Thomas, Peter Blake, George Michael, Status Quo's Francis Rossi and Rick Parfitt, Culture Club's Jon Moss and Boy George, Sting, Frankie Goes to Hollywood's Holly, Paul McCartney, and David Bowie.

On the day of the song's recording, the world's media attended, hence world coverage was guaranteed, but this did not fare well with Margaret Thatcher's government who at the time who refused to waive VAT on sales. However, following a much publicised debate, she relented and donated the tax back. Once recorded, "Do They Know It's Christmas?" was dispatched to pressing plants to be released by Phonogram Records on 3 December 1984. BBC Radio 1 played the single each hour, a move followed by stations up and down the

UK. It entered the singles chart at the pole position, where it stayed for five weeks. The promotional video was screened across all the television stations on music shows and news programmes. Record sales across the world hit an all-time high, including the USA where it sold in excess of one million copies.

The Band Aid Trust was set up to handle the finances generated by record sales estimated at £8 million, and to cash in on the single's world dominance, plans for a duel-venue concert began to generate more money. Once again it was the brainchild of Bob Geldof and Midge Ure, who planned to stage two concerts one after the other on 13 July at Wembley Stadium in London, then the John F Kennedy Stadium in Philadelphia. The concert, "Live Aid" - billed as the Global Jukebox - far exceeded all expectations. It was the concert to end all concerts which raised an estimated £150 million, was talked about in glowing terms for the years that followed. The UK leg was introduced by the Coldstream Guards, followed by Status Quo.

Other acts included: The Boomtown Rats, Bryan Ferry, Dire Straits, David Bowie, Elton John, Queen, Paul McCartney, Sade, Paul Young, Elvis Costello, Sting, Phil Collins (who appeared at the Wembley Stadium and the Kennedy Stadium) and The Who. The US contingent that followed featured acts like the Four Tops, The Beach Boys, Simple Minds, The Pretenders, Madonna, Tina Turner, Mick Jagger, Patti Labelle, Bob Dylan, and Hall & Oates. The concerts represented the largest scale satellite link up across the world, with an estimated audience of 1.9 billion across 150 nations. Throughout the concerts – which were televised in their entirety for later commercial video release - 300 telephone lines were manned by BBC staff, and seven hours into the London concert, £1.2 million had been raised by credit card donations.

Bob Geldof was criticised for failing to include black artists in the Band Aid project, but he claimed that while organising the Live Aid concert he did attempt to persuade leading African-American acts to take part. At the end of the day, he said, the concert was to raise money for a starving nation, not about the artist roster.

Greatly encouraged by the success of "Do They Know It's Christmas?", various Band Aid style incarnations began to emerge, such as Starvation which featured reggae/pop acts like Madness, General Public and UB40. Disco Aid with dance music acts including Phil Fearon, Jaki Graham, Hazell Dean and DJ Steve Walsh; Northern Lights, comprising Canadian super groups released "Tears Are Not Enough". And USA For Africa's "We Are The World" charity single written by Michael Jackson and Lionel Richie, who, alongside fifties calypso star Harry Belafonte, were inspired by the UK's blueprint single to organise a similar super US act ensemble of American artists.

A year following "Do They Know It's Christmas?", a twelve inch single, with an extended mix, was released. This time messages from artists participating in the original recording were included. This version peaked at number three in the UK chart. And, five years later, with an altered line-up, an updated version was recorded. The positive legacy of Band Aid still stands.

(See also Christmas 1989 and 2004).

UK CHRISTMAS NUMBER ONES 1952-2022

1985

MERRY CHRISTMAS EVERYONE/ WITH MY HEART
SHAKIN' STEVENS

The most charted singles act in the UK chart during the 1980s was not Madonna, Michael Jackson or Duran Duran, but a Welshman born in Cardiff on 4 March 1948 as Michael Barratt, who became Shakin' Stevens, an Elvis Presley/Gene Vincent cloned rock 'n' roll stylist. His knee bends, crotch swivels and lip curls had been practised to perfection!

He was one of twelve children who were raised in a rock 'n' roll environment thanks to his brothers' musical tastes. So, it was not surprising when in 1968 Michael Barratt joined his first group The Sunsets who rocked their way through the club circuit until 1970. With a name change to Shakin' Stevens and The Sunsets, they signed to EMI Records' Parlophone label. They recorded the album "A Legend", with Dave Edmunds at his own studio Rockfield in Wales. Carrying a 1950s style, the album flopped, likewise the extracted single "Down On The Farm". Parlophone dropped them, so a year later, the group signed with CBS Records, where they released the "I'm No JD" album which also flopped.

Shakin' Stevens and The Sunsets continued singing by making a name for themselves as a touring group, mostly across Europe. Due to their success on the Continent, Dureco Records in Holland offered them a recording deal. They then recorded for several labels, including Pink Elephant where they released their last single as a group titled "Jungle Rock" in 1976.

With no recording contract Shakin' Stevens turned to acting. In 1977 he made his West End debut as one of three actors playing Elvis Presley in Jack Good's adaptation of the icon's life. This won the Best Musical of 1977 Theatre Award. His success on stage led to him signing a solo recording deal with Track Records. His one year stay there was unsuccessful as his self titled debut solo album, and three extracted singles failed to chart. The following year, Shakin' Stevens was a regular performer on Jack Good's revival of his 1950s UK television show Oh Boy!, and this lead to a new recording deal with CBS/Epic Records. He had an uninspiring start with a trio of flop singles – "Treat Her Right", "Endless Sleep" and "Spooky".

UK CHRISTMAS NUMBER ONES 1952-2022

In early 1980, "Hot Dog" was his very belated chart debut. It peaked in the top thirty. It took awhile, but finally Shakin' Stevens was on his way. The single's follow-up was his version of The Blasters' "Marie Marie", a UK top twenty hit. Most of Stevens' future work would be cover versions of tried and tested songs. And his first chart topper, "This Ole House" was a good example, as it had been a 1954 number one title for Rosemary Clooney. "You Drive Me Crazy", an original composition from Ronnie Harwood, followed to hit the top two. But his second number one was on the horizon with "Green Door", previously recorded by Frankie Vaughan, with "It's Raining" following, a top ten entrant.

In 1982, the denim-clad rock 'n' roller released his own composition "Oh Julie" – his third chart topper. He was a consistent charter during the next two years with cover version singles like "Shirley" (John Fred and His Playboy Band), "I'll Be Satisfied" (Jackie Wilson) and "Blue Christmas" (Elvis Presley). Early in 1984 he duetted with female rocker and fellow Welsh native Bonnie Tyler – the result of the collaboration was a revival of the Dinah Washington & Brook Benton 1960 duet hit "A Rockin' Good Way (To Mess Around And Fall In Love)"; number five UK hit.

The solo Shakin' Stevens' "A Love Worth Waiting For" returned him to the top five, with two further top ten singles "A Letter to You" and "Teardrops" following. His "Breaking Up My Heart" started 1985, with the Dave Edmunds' production "Lipstick, Powder And Paint" next, which reached the UK top twenty. However, the best was yet to come when Shakin' Stevens beat off the chart's dominating names like Prince and Madonna to dominate the Christmas list with "Merry Christmas Everyone", written by Bob Heattie and produced by Dave Edmunds. The intention had been to release it in 1984 but Shakin' Stevens did not want to detract sales from Band Aid's charity release "Do They Know It's Christmas". Like the latter version, Stevens' single has re-charted several times, and is naturally regularly included on Christmas compilations.

A pair of top twenty singles – "Turning Away" and "Because I Love You" ensured Steven's presence in 1986. The following year he charted four times, with "What Do you Want To Make Those Eyes At Me For?" (Emile Ford And The Checkmates) reaching the highest position at number five. By the time he reached the 1990s, his career took a noticeable nosedive. Of all his single releases, only two managed to reach the top thirty – his version of The Detroit Emeralds' "Feel The Need In Me", and "Love Attack". He also recorded a further pair of Festive singles: the 1990 "The Best Christmas Of Them All" and 1991's "I'll Be Home This Christmas". Top twenty and top forty entrants respectively. His final UK hit under his original Epic Recording contract, "Radio" in 1992, featured Queen's Roger Taylor, and stalled at number 37.

In 2002 Stevens was convicted of drunk driving, while professionally his career gained momentum again in 2005 with the release of his "Greatest Hits" album, a top five hit. He also participated in Peter Kay's number one charity single "Is This The Way To Amarillo", and won the television reality programme Hit Me Baby One More Time, against fellow 80s artists like Shalamar, Tiffany and T 'Pau's Carol Decker. This led to a brief interest in his career once more when Virgin/EMI Records released his version of Pink's "Trouble".

In 2008 he opened the Glastonbury Festival, followed by a UK tour. Two years later he suffered a heart attack brought on by the stress of working on a new album. Happily, Stevens fully recovered to embark upon his 30th Anniversary tour.

As of this writing (2023), Shaky released the "Re-Set" album which peaked at number 24 on the UK album chart.

Shakin' Stevens might have been a late starter in the UK chart stakes but to date to his credit he has enjoyed 33 top forty hits. He also has the distinction of being the UK's biggest singles seller during the 1980s, and he deserves respect for defying cultural convention by sticking to his winning formula of updating rock 'n' roll.

1986

REET PETITE (THE SWEETEST GIRL IN TOWN)/ YOU BROUGHT A CHANGE IN ME/ I'M THE ONE TO DO IT
JACKIE WILSON

Exactly a year on from a Welsh retro-rocker's Christmas chart topper, and closely approaching the one decade anniversary of rock 'n' roll's crowned king's demise, one of R&B's unsung heroes enjoyed a revived interest. Sadly, he wasn't alive to experience his unexpected good fortune.

Jackie Wilson was born (as Jack Wilson) in Detroit, Michigan, on 9 June 1934, and spent most of his early years absorbing the music of The Mills Brothers and Mario Lanza, and blues artists like Muddy Waters and Roy Brown. He was also greatly influenced by the choir at a nearby Billups Chapel. Like many teenagers, Jackie Wilson began his working life as a boxer, winning the American Amateur Golden Gloves Welterweight title under the name 'Sonny Wilson'. It was during this period that Jackie met fellow Detroiter and boxer Berry Gordy Jr who, like himself, had ambitions in the music industry. He later headed up Motown Records, the most influential black-owned record company in the history of music. Regularly at odds with the authorities, Jackie had been incarcerated in a juvenile detention centre twice, and at the age of seventeen, he was married and a father.

Jackie Wilson's boxing career came to an abrupt end, however, when he decided to heed his mother's advice and complete his education. He went on to graduate from the Highland Park High School. During the day he worked on the assembly line in a Detroit car factory, while at night and at weekends he pursued his love of music by performing at local night spots as a soloist before forming The Falcons that included in the membership his cousin, the future lead singer with the Four Tops – Levi Stubbs. Jackie also did the rounds of entering talent shows, and at one held at his local Paradise Theatre, King Records' Johnny Otis chanced to be in the audience. He arranged for him to join The Thrillers, later known as The Royals and eventually The Midnighters. He then met Billy Ward who encouraged him to replace The Dominoes' lead singer Clyde McPhatter, and as such he recorded several singles during the group's tenure including 1956's "St Therese Of The Roses." A year later he had left the group to pursue a solo career. He yearned for solo success, and inspired by Elvis Presley's personal admiration for him and with advice from leading Detroit agent and publisher Al Green, who became his manager, a unique solo deal was struck with Brunswick Records, a subsidiary of Decca Records. When Al Green died suddenly, Nat Tarnopol replaced him as Jackie's manager, and his first hit under the new deal was "Reet Petite (The Sweetest Girl In Town)".

Motown Records' founder Berry Gordy wrote the song with his sister Gwen, and cousin, Billy Davis, to become a mid selling US single in 1957, but a number seven UK hit. And it was this same single that shot into the UK pole position, 29 years after its original release. This upbeat release sold over 700,000 copies over the Christmas period, aided, no doubt, by its clay animated promotional video, directed by the London-based Giblets company and first shown on a BBC2's Arena documentary programme. "Reet Petite" dominated the UK chart for four weeks. Incidentally, an 'Extended Shock' sub-titled dance remix of the tune dominated both UK twelve inch and dance music sales charts. A revived interest in Jackie Wilson and his music was well and truly beginning! The tragedy was that Jackie had died nearly three years earlier.

Following the original release of "Reet Petite" in 1957, Jackie Wilson went on to score further hits with "To Be Loved", a top thirty hit on both sides of the Atlantic. "We Have Love"and "Lonely Teardrops" followed. The latter single topped the US R&B chart in 1958, later crossing onto the mainstream listing top ten, selling in excess of one million copies at the time. "That's Why" and "I'll Be Satisfied" – the last song to be co-penned by Berry Gordy - and "You Better Know It" sustained the singer's high profile in the US as a charting name. Jackie Wilson was a rising star and when he began performing in the white nightclubs of Las Vegas and New York, he knew he could not fail. He was loved for his electric stage shows, often racy and frenetic, which regularly included him jumping into women's arms, having his shirt pulled from his back, and being escorted off stage before he was mobbed. This, and his impeccable dress style, earned him the title Mr Excitement. His showmanship, of course, was later emulated by Michael Jackson and James Brown.

Between the late 1950s and mid 1960s, Jackie Wilson stood alongside the best America had on offer by way of popular black vocalists. However, that could so easily have come to a sudden halt when in 1961 he was shot in the back and stomach by a fan waiting for him in his New York apartment.

He lost a kidney and a bullet was lodged in his spine. It took Wilson two years to recover. In 1969 he enjoyed his second biggest selling UK single with "Your Love Keeps Lifting Me) Higher And Higher", a number one hit, followed by "I Get The Sweetest Feeling", a top ten entrant in 1972. Three years later the two titles were released as a double A-side to peak in the top thirty. Jackie Wilson's career came to a sudden halt in September 1975 when he collapsed from a heart attack while on stage during a Dick Clark promoted Good Ol' Rock 'N' Roll Revue. His audience believed it to be part of his act, so no-one acted immediately.

When a member of The Coasters (who were also on the bill) realised Wilson wasn't breathing because he had hit his head while falling, he managed to resuscitate him before he was rushed to a local hospital. The fall left him with severe brain damage. Wilson regained consciousness following four months in a coma, but never fully recovered. To pay for his hospitalisation, Barry White and other fellow soul acts, performed benefit concerts to raise the necessary funds. Despite having earned an estimated $200 million during his career, the singer was penniless which meant that much of the money raised went directly to the IRS to cover unpaid taxes.

Just shy of his 50th birthday in January 1984, Jackie Wilson died in a New Jersey nursing home. His nine-year struggle for life was over. His funeral was held at Detroit's Chrysler Drive Baptist Church and was attended by Berry Gordy and other Motown acts, while his grave was unmarked, being identified simply as B261 in the West Lawn Cemetery until 1987 when sufficient money was raised to buy a headstone befitting the star that he was. If the 1975 tragedy had never happened, Jackie Wilson would no doubt have been able to promote and enjoy the renewed interest in his music, in much the same way as Ben E King or James Brown did. He was part of the veteran contingent of classic soul acts whose work was given a new lease of life by the Great British record buyers, irrespective of its age.

Until 2022 "Reet Petite (The Sweetest Girl In Town)" held the record for the longest time between its debut in the chart to its eventual peak on the UK singles chart - 29 years and 42 days to be precise. It was overtaken by Kate Bush's "Running Up That Hill (A Deal With God)".

The once unmarked grave now has a headstone that reads "No More Lonely Teardrops".

A fitting epitaph for one of music's 'lost' artists.

UK CHRISTMAS NUMBER ONES 1952-2022

1987

ALWAYS ON MY MIND/ DO I HAVE TO?
PET SHOP BOYS

This year was indeed a retro twelve months in popular music. It witnessed high profile comebacks from established acts like Tom Jones, George Harrison and Labi Siffre, and re-issues from Ben E King, Percy Sledge and Nina Simone, while opening on last Christmas' hangover – "Reet Petite (The Sweetest Girl In Town)" from Jackie Wilson.

Sandwiched between T'Pau's rock ballad "China In Your Hand" and Belinda Carlisle's breakthrough single "Heaven Is A Place On Earth", was this year's Festive chart topper, a version of a well-known song lifted from a television show.

Born on 10 July 1954 in Gosforth, Tyne and Wear, Neil Francis Tennant joined the folk band Dust before graduating from North London's Polytechnic. He intended to study Imperial and Commonwealth history but instead answered an advertisement in the UK Press Gazette for a production manager for Marvel Comics. Part of his job was interviewing artists - his first was with Marc Bolan – and host launch parties. Neil also befriended Tom Watkins, then manager of the group Giggles, but who would later on manage the Pet Shop Boys!

Born on 4 October 1959 in Blackpool, Lancashire, Christopher Sean Lowe joined the seven-man group One Under The Eight as keyboardist. He also studied theoretical architecture at Liverpool University.

In 1981, Neil Tennant and Christopher Lowe met by chance in a record shop in King's Road, London. They started talking about music, discovered they had a common interest and decided to join forces. After recording a handful of demo tracks in a Camden studio, they hiked the tapes around record companies. At this point they called themselves West End, later changing it to the Pet Shop Boys after a bunch of their friends who worked in an Ealing pet shop.

Two years later when Neil Tennant was in New York interviewing Bobby 'O' Orlando for Smash Hits magazine for whom he now worked. The two also collaborated in the recording studio, resulting in the release of "West End Girls" which had previously been rejected by UK companies. After a sluggish start, the single (released by Epic) became a big seller across Europe, thanks

UK CHRISTMAS NUMBER ONES 1952-2022

to the emergence of the Hi-NRG cult following, and a reworking of the single (this time when the duo were signed to EMI) shot to the UK pole position in early 1986. It stayed there for two weeks, selling 750,000 copies, and went on to win a BRIT award for Best Single of the Year, an Ivor Novello Award for International Hit of the Year, plus other honours. The single also topped the US chart, their only one, and by the end of the single's life had sold one million copies across the world, spreading the musical word of the Pet Shop Boys' distinctive blend of synthesised music and vocal harmony which was immediately adopted by a huge gay following before crossing into the mainstream market. Their "Please" album was next to peak at number three.

"Love Comes Quickly" was next, but stalled at number nine, but before 1986 closed, the Pet Shop Boys enjoyed a pair of top ten hits with "Opportunities (Let's Make Lots Of Money)" and "Suburbia" – so named after the film. Their next chart topper followed in 1987 with "It's A Sin", originally written for Miquel Brown and/or Divine. To accompany all their single releases, the duo produced innovative promotional videos and it was these, as well as their music, that ensured their future was secure. They were a highly profitable business proposition yet, to date, they had not stepped onto a concert stage!

During 1987 the Pet Shop Boys fulfilled a personal ambition by working with one of their idols, Dusty Springfield, collaborating on "What Have I Done To Deserve This?". Resisting the concerns of the record company, The single soared to number two in both the UK and the USA, returning Dusty to the public spotlight after several years due to her low-profile living in the USA. It was a tremendous reunion and comeback for the UK's much loved singer and led to a second string of future hits for her into the 90s. The duo released their next album "Actually", following the release of "Rent" and their next UK chart topper "Always On My Mind" in 1987. Originally recorded by Gwen McCrae and Brenda Lee in 1972, the song gave a top ten hit to Elvis Presley, while Willie Nelson's version in 1982 was a Grammy award winner. The Pet Shop Boys had performed their version on the television show "Love Me Tender", screened to mark the tenth anniversary of Elvis' death when, due to limited timing, plans to do a dance version of 'Baby, Let's Play House' were scrapped in favour of 'Always On My Mind'. It was so well received by the viewing audience, that "Always On My Mind" was scheduled for single release and it shot to the top spot, to stay for four weeks. A re-recorded version was included on their next album "Introspective". The Pet Shop Boys stamped their own Hi-NRG mark on the song which was alienated from the anything released previously. It is well documented that The Pogues' "Fairytale Of New York" was denied the UK pole position because of the duo's domination. The group's guest vocalist, the late Kirsty McColl said at the time that she liked the song, Pogues' Shane McGowan was less charitable!

By this time they were already one of the world's top selling singles acts of the mid/late 1980s, no doubt helped by their updated yet anglicised and electronic emulation of American soul-disco music.

Further hits arrived during the next year – the UK number one titled "Heart" (intended initially for the dance diva Hazell Dean), and two top ten hits "Domino Dancing" and "Left To My Own Devices". Two months after "Heart", the Pet Shop Boys were persuaded to perform, with other acts, at a charity concert staged at Manchester's Piccadilly Theatre, while their first movie "It Couldn't Happen Here" hit the cinema circuit in July 1988.

The next year, the Pet Shop Boys worked again with Dusty Springfield, this time producing "Nothing Has Been Proved", a track from the soundtrack of "Scandal", which told the story of the Profumo affair. They later collaborated on Dusty's celebrated comeback album "Reputation" and the duo toured the UK, playing before standing-room-only audiences, who delighted at their imaginative use of visual projections and costume changes which complimented their music. The tour crossed the UK before transferring to Japan, one of their most lucrative markets. Also this year, the duo worked with their second female vocalist – Liza Minnelli. The result was her first UK hit single, "Losing My Mind", extracted from her "Results" album to reach the UK top ten in 1989, the album also went on to produce two further minor hits "Don't Drop Bombs" and "So Sorry I Said".

Throughout the 1990s, the Pet Shop Boys were regular chart names but by the end of 1991 it was apparent they were losing their punch, their music becoming too predictable. However, in mid-1993, they returned with renewed vigour with the top ten UK hit "Can You Forgive Her" and their version of the Village People's 1979 hit "Go West", while their album "Very" re-established them as a chart topping name. Alongside recording commitments, the Pet Shop Boys continued to tour, albeit irregularly, ensuring their name stayed in the public arena. Although they were unable to secure another chart topper (to date), the duo enjoyed regular chart success through the entire decade, including the top ten hit "Absolutely Fabulous" recorded with the main performers on the BBC TV show, namely Jennifer Saunders and Joanna Lumley. All proceeds went to Comic Relief.

In 2003, they launched two new labels – Olde English Vinyl and Lucky Kunst – following the demise of their original label, Spaghetti. A year later, after performing a free concert with the Dresdner Orchestra, in London's Trafalgar Square, they headlined the Moscow Live 8 Concert in Red Square. In 2006 they worked with Robbie Williams on his "Rudebox" album, before embarking upon a world tour. Three years later, several singles were extracted from the "Love Etc" album, and once again hit the touring trail across the globe. Their live album/dvd package "Pandemonium" was issued in 2010, followed by a 'greatest hits' compilation and "Format, a collection of their flipsides covering 1996-2009. Joining other stars, the Pet Shop Boys were asked to perform "West Side Girls" during the closing ceremony of the 2012 Olympic Games. And in 2013 left EMI Records' Parlophone label, after 28 years, to join Kobalt Label Services for their 12th studio album "Electric", pressed on their own x2 label.

In 2023, they announced that they had started recording (with producer James Ford) their fifteenth studio album .

As of writing, this world famous UK electronic pop duo had sold over 50 million records worldwide, were Grammy nominees six times, and three time winners at the BRIT awards. Their avant garde fashion, state of the art computer technology and transformation into futuristic visionaries, ensured the Pet Shop Boys are as popular today as they were in 1985.

1988

MISTLETOE AND WINE/ MARMADUKE/ TRUE LOVE WAYS
CLIFF RICHARD

A little known song featured in the little known musical Scraps, was an adaptation of Hans Christian Anderson's The Little Match Girl set in Victorian London. One of the song's co-writers, Keith Strachan (with Jeremy Paul and Leslie Stewart) believed the song was a hit record but needed someone to record it. Scraps was renamed, adapted for television in 1987 and featured Jimmy Jewell, Roger Daltrey and Twiggy. When "Mistletoe And Wine" was originally composed, it carried a different message to that recorded by Cliff Richard.

The writers intended it to sound like a Christmas carol being sung while the little match girl is made homeless in the snow by an uncaring couple. When the musical was shown on television, "Mistletoe And Wine" had become a pub song, sung by the local prostitute as portrayed by Twiggy,. When Cliff heard the song, he loved it but wanted to change the lyrics to reflect the real Christmas feeling. When the writers agreed, the single became his twelfth UK chart topper, spending four weeks in the pole position, selling in excess of 750,000 copies, to become the best selling single of 1988. It was also his 99th chart single.

Naturally, Cliff promoted the catchy ballad and could be seen in a small group of people, dressed for the snow, swaying their heads, smiling and singing, mesmerised by the melody. It had been twenty seven long years since Cliff dominated the Christmas top spot, yet the festive season was always associated with him, whether via a new release or a re-issue. Should he release a new single, bookies would lay down odds of him being in the number one slot – a practice that has occurred for many years now.

Once again, it seemed he could do no wrong. His career continued to hit new heights. His double album "Private Collection" passed quadruple platinum status, with sales in excess of one million. In 1989, he was honoured at the BRIT Awards ceremony for his Outstanding Contribution to British Music, and he released his 100th single titled "The Best Of Me", a number two hit. He staged Cliff Richard: The Event at Wembley Stadium, then went on to record a Stock, Aitken and Waterman composition/production "I Just Don't Have The Heart", before duetting with Van Morrison on "Whenever God Shines His Light".

The new decade dawned and Cliff the singer, entertainer and celebrity, rose to greater heights. His Access All Areas '92 tour spanned thirteen sold out dates that included an unprecedented 13 dates at Wembley Arena. In October 1985, Cliff visited Buckingham Palace where he received a knighthood from the Queen for his tireless charity work and his contribution to the entertainment world. He already had an OBE.

Before the release of his next Christmas number one, Cliff Richard fulfilled am ambition he had nurtured since the 1960s.

(See also Christmas 1960 and 1990)

1989

DO THEY KNOW IT'S CHRISTMAS?/ DO THEY KNOW IT'S CHRISTMAS INSTRUMENTAL
BAND AID II

Half a decade after the original "Do They Know It's Christmas", a new version was recorded, this time produced by the Hit Factory team, Stock, Aitken and Waterman. Five years down the line from the first single, a follow up was needed and, as recording stars who were big at the time took part in the original, it was expected that recording acts that dominated the singles charts of the late 1980s were to take part in raising awareness about the less fortunate in East Africa.

Orchestrated by Bob Geldof & Midge Ure, 'Do They Know It's Christmas?' mark II was produced, arranged & assembled by by the Hit Factory team, Stock, Aitken and Waterman and obviously their leading acts Kylie Minogue, Jason Donovan, Big Fun & Sonia did partake in that version, alongside Cliff Richard, Bananarama (for the second time), Technotronic, Wet Wet Wet, Jimmy Sommerville, Bros, Chris Rea, Kevin Godley, D Mob, Cathy Dennis and soul music acts such as The Pasadenas, Lisa Stansfield & Glen Goldsmith. Once again, all proceeds from the single's release were earmarked to provide famine relief.

Topping the chart for three weeks in total, this version was released by Polydor Records. Despite the charitable intention behind Band Aid II, rock pundits dismissed it because the original single attracted big named acts at the time, and while this new line-up was impressive, it paled by comparison, lacking artist credibility.

It was also felt that the 1989 version lacked the passion of its predecessor, but perhaps this situation would have been remedied if the big charting acts of the era like say, Rick Astley, Soul II Soul, Transvision Vamp or T'Pau had been included. Nonetheless, this version still hit the UK pole position over the Christmas period, raising much needed funds which, ultimately was the aim of the Band Aid projects.

Regrettably, regardless of the line up, Band Aid II lacked the across-the-board appeal enjoyed by its prototype, and was never held in the same high regard, as was proven by its reissue one year later when it failed to chart.

(See also Christmas 1984 and 2004)

1990

SAVIOUR'S DAY/ THE 'OH BOY' MEDLEY
CLIFF RICHARD

Welcome to Cliff Richard in the 1990s! From the previous year's hangover of the Van Morrison duet "Whenever God Shines His Light" still in the chart, coupled with Band Aid II's revival of "Do They Know It's Christmas", on which he sang, the 'Peter Pan Of Pop' released his first proper hit of the decade. The dance slanted "Stronger Than That", supported by serious clubland fans thanks to its funkier phrased remixes, helped elevate it into the UK top twenty. His version of Bette Midler's "From A Distance" also hit the top twenty, while his revival of Herman Hermits' classic "Silhouettes" peaked in the top ten, and 'Christmas Cliff' was about to strike again.

During the release and subsequent yuletide dominance of "Saviour's Day", Cliff Richard was on (what seemed to be) an eternal roll. His 38-date From A Distance tour was a complete success, with the live album of the same name hitting the UK top five. Radio and television exposure was planned to ensure the single was this year's Christmas song, because, by now, EMI Records played up to the public expectation of an obligatory single from Cliff, and 1990's title let no-one down.

"Saviour's Day" was premiered on a television special celebrating the success of the UK soap Coronation Street, and supported by Cliff on live dates and a constant media rotation of promotion. However, the song very nearly didn't happen. If Cliff's friend Chris Eaton had been unsuccessful in convincing the singer that the song was perfect for Christmas release, "From A Distance" would have taken its place. "Saviour's Day" ended up being wedged between white US rapper Vanilla Ice, and UK heavy metal merchants, Iron Maiden - eclectic indeed! - and was voted both the Best and Worst Christmas single by record buyers. Chris Eaton later wrote "Santa's List" for Cliff which became a top three hit in 2003.

As mentioned previously, Cliff fulfilled a long time ambition to play Heathcliff. In 1996 he joined the cast of the Tim Rice/John Farrar musical adaption of the Emily Bronte novel. Cliff invested $2 million into the project, capacity-filled theatres across the UK watched the musical during a six month tour. He worked with a fitness trainer to ensure a healthy body weight of 11st 8lb with a noticeable half-stone of muscle added to his chest, legs and biceps.

A further year of celebration loomed in 1998 when Sir Cliff Richard celebrated forty years in the music business. To mark the occasion he issued "Can't Keep This Feeling In", from the "Real As I Wanna Be" album. It is true to say, Cliff's career started to slow down but every so often he would hit the headlines once more. One such time was the surprise announcement that he was leaving his long time label EMI Records to move first to Papillion, then on to the reactivated Decca label. From there, he returned to his 'home' at EMI.

Following the acquisition/merger/reconstruction of EMI Records within Universal Music, and due to European regulators, several notable EMI signings including Cliff, David Bowie, Pink Floyd and Kate Bush, were transferred to rival company, Warner Music, as part of the Parlophone label divestment sale by Universal to Warner Music. It will take some getting used to Cliff being handled now by one of America's leading major media corporations.

Cliff Richard is now the third top selling singles artist in the UK, with sales in excess of 21 million, and 250 million worldwide. He is now as much a part of Britain's heritage as the royal family. He continues to be featured in most high profile functions and his UK tours are instant sell-outs thanks to his legions of loyal fans who have either grown up with him, or been attracted to him by a particular single. He is also probably one of the most decorated artists for his services to popular music, with a raft of awards, honours and certificates. He is also a selfless contributor to a variety of charities, and since the mid-1960s has given one tenth of his income to charitable causes.

Through the Cliff Richard Charitable Trust, he has financed grants that benefit fifty different UK organisations working with children and the elderly, and medical research. He also raised awareness of dementia, by supporting the UK's Alzheimer's Research facilities. He has also been hands-on in countries like Bangladesh and Uganda, and makes personal appearances at homes and hospitals catering for special needs children. He is also a business man of considerable note, owning, among other things, his own brand of wine. Establishing the Cliff Richard Tennis Foundation to encourage primary schools in the UK to include the sport in their criteria, and to this end hundreds of thousands of school children participate in tennis sessions that tour the UK. His Foundation is now affiliated to the Lawn Tennis Association. Naturally, he is a regular visitor to Wimbledon where, if the weather is bad, he instigates singalongs for the other attendees. And, he remains very much in demand as an artist.

Yes, the world would be a much poorer place without Sir Cliff!

In August 2014 Cliff Richard's Berkshire home was searched by the South Yorkshire Police following a tip off that he had assaulted a young boy during a Sheffield appearance by the American preacher Billy Graham during 1985. Cliff was in Portugal at the time of the police raid but voluntarily returned to the UK for police questioning. At the time of writing, the Crown Prosecution Service announced that due to lack of evidence, Cliff Richard will not face charges related to historical sexual abuse claims. Sir Cliff Richard thereafter announced plans to launch a comeback to help put the episode behind him including a Christmas timed album and despite legal claims against the BBC, the corporation plans to be part of the comeback salvage as will Sony Music who released the comeback project "Just......Fabulous Rock 'n' Roll" which restored his standing as a top five selling album artist. Subsequently he was scooped up by Warner Records for future recording projects.

(See also Christmas 1960 and 1988)

1991

BOHEMIAN RHAPSODY/ THESE ARE THE DAYS OF OUR LIVES
QUEEN

Queen returned to top the 1991 Christmas period with the same single released sixteen years earlier. But this time around it was a more poignant release, and sadly under tragic circumstances. By this time the group were stadium superstars, iconic figureheads with their music continuing to selling by the million.

Following their 1976 album "A Day At The Races", Queen returned with "News Of The World" a year later, featuring the anthemic "We Are The Champions" and "We Will Rock You", released as a double A-sided single. The album peaked at number four, while the single hit the top two. Despite the united public front, Queen was fragmenting, with rumours of a pending break up. However, the music continued. With fifty naked girls cycling around Wimbledon Stadium, the group advertised their next single "Bicycle Race" and "Fat Bottomed Girls", tracks extracted from their seventh album "Jazz". During 1979 and between their sell-out arena tours, they were asked to compose the soundtrack for the science fiction film "Flash Gordon", followed by "The Game" album from which "Play The Game" and "Another One Bites The Dust" were extracted for single release.

Through the 1980s Queen continued to enjoy a high profile on record and stage, and following a greatest hits compilation, their next studio album, the more dance/R&B inspired "Hot Space" was released, containing the famous duet between Freddie Mercury and a visiting David Bowie titled "Under Pressure". During 1984 "Radio Ga Ga" was lifted from "The Works" album, accompanied by one of the group's most exciting videos with scenes from the film "Metropolis" being interspersed between the group's performance. "I Want To Break Free" was the album's next single where Queen members dressed as characters seemingly inspired by ITV's long running soap "Coronation Street". A moustached Freddie wearing a tight black mini-skirt and outsized false breasts, brandishing a vacuum around a living room, springs to mind! Their workload never wavered as in between world touring, Queen continued to record, with the albums "One Vision" , "A Kind Of Magic" and "The Miracle" released before the close of the decade. By this time Freddie Mercury's health was giving cause for concern. He was unable to fulfil the group's ongoing gruelling commitments, yet despite his failing health, he satisfied a long-standing personal ambition by recording with the opera star Montserrat Caballe a song he had penned named "Barcelona". Following this project, it was apparent Freddie was a very sick man indeed. In 1991 Queen released the "Innuendo" album and single: both hit the UK top. Shortly after this, Freddie appeared in what was to be his last promotional video – "These Are The Days Of Our Lives". Filmed in black and white, the video showed a desperately ill singer. On 23 November 1991 he announced to the world that he had AIDS. He died the next day at his Kensington home.

Following Freddie's funeral, it was revealed that he had donated all rights to "Bohemian Rhapsody" to the Terrence Higgins Trust, an AIDS charity that he had supported in life. EMI Records honoured his last wish that the song with "These Are The Days Of My Life" should be issued as a single. This time the song topped the UK Christmas chart for five weeks, initially earning the Terrence Higgins Trust over £1 million. In April 1992 the Freddie Mercury Tribute Concert was staged at Wembley Stadium before an estimated 72,000 strong audience. Stars like Elton John, David Bowie, George Michael and Annie Lennox were among the participating acts in a concert broadcast to 70 countries and watched by one billion people. Following this gala the Mercury Phoenix Trust was founded through which the concert money could be distributed.

Following Freddie's death, there was a natural upsurge in sales of his solo work like his self-named album from which "In My Defence", "The Great Pretender" and "Living On My Own" were taken for single release; the latter (in a dance remix form) hitting the UK pole position in 1993. Queen albums were also in demand again, with sales passing twenty million. However, there was one more project to come featuring Freddie as lead vocalist. Four years after his death and following months of remixing, the "Made In Heaven" album was issued. Naturally, it topped the UK chart, and spawned three singles – "Heaven For Everyone" (UK number two), "A Winter's Tale" (number six) and the original version of Brian May's cover "Too Much Love Will Kill You" (number five).

At the 1992 BRITS ceremony held at London's Hammersmith Odeon, "Bohemian Rhapsody" won the Best British Single, while Freddie Mercury was posthumously honoured with the Outstanding Contribution To British Music award. In the US, "Bohemian Rhapsody" was heavily featured in the film "Wayne's World", and re-released to peak at number two with all royalties going to the Earvin 'Magic Johnson AIDS Foundation'.

Briefly into the mid-1990s, both Brian May and Roger Taylor released solo work with varying degrees of success. During 2002 the rock theatrical "We Will Rock You" opened at the Dominion Theatre in London's West End. Written by author/comedian Ben Elton, the production featured Queen's best known material. It was due to close in 2014. In 2004, Brian May and Roger Taylor joined forces to bring Queen back to the concert stage. With Paul Rodgers (ex lead singer with Free and Bad Company) joining them, he was not a replacement for Freddie Mercury but more a vocal addition. The group was billed as Paul Rodgers with Queen. John Deacon, who had retired from the business, did not join them.

In 2010 the rights to Queen's entire recording output for EMI Records had expired. Universal Records acquired the rights, with the sole intention of re-mastering, re-packaging and re-releasing the music. A revamped "Greatest Hits" compilation was the first from this new relationship. And two years later, Queen performed at the closing ceremony of the Summer Olympics held in London. A backdrop of a re-mastered video clip showing Freddie Mercury performing his call/response routine from their 1986 Wembley Stadium concert, was an unexpected wow factor!

'Bohemian Rhapsody' is the only Christmas charttopper to be a UK number one in four calender years (1975-76/1991-92). EMI would later be acquired and restructured within the Universal Music set-up, bringing Queen's recordings full circle within the newly created Universal EMI Music.

Virgin Records currently globally distribute and re-issue all things Queen.

Queen as of this writing are still persist as an active unit, though without their flamboyant showman.

(See also Christmas 1975)

UK CHRISTMAS NUMBER ONES 1952-2022

1992

I WILL ALWAYS LOVE YOU/ JESUS LOVES ME
WHITNEY HOUSTON

This powerhouse of a ballad first started its life as a country and western song, written and performed by Dolly Parton, no less. She recorded her version in 1973, and one of the most exciting soul artists to emerge from the US recorded her take in 1992 for the film "Bodyguard" starring Kevin Costner. "I Will Always Love You" set the world on fire. It topped the UK chart for ten weeks, the longest run ever for a female soloist, and sales passed platinum status twice. International success equalled, and often surpassed, that in the UK, where it sold over 1.5 million copies, elevating it to the tenth top selling single of the 1990s.

Born into a gospel background on 9 August 1963 in Newark, New Jersey (died 11 February 2012), Whitney Houston's Emily 'Cissy' Houston was a noted member of the gospel group the Drinkard Sisters. She later fronted the Sweet Inspirations who recorded for Atlantic Records and backed many recording artists on studio sessions including Elvis Presley. With her aunts Dionne and Dee Dee Warwick, Whitney spent most of her young life surrounded by music whether listening to it on the radio, watching artists like Aretha Franklin record in the studio, or singing alongside her mother on stage where, more often than not, she would sing "The Greatest Love Of All" from "The Greatest" film, depicting the life story of Muhammad Ali.

Whitney joined the CLICK model agency where, as a seventeen-year-old, she was photographed for the covers of glossy magazines, leading to a contract with Revlon. In time, the work bored her, so she took acting lessons in New York which would benefit her when she performed. Blessed with both a soulful vocal range of one much older, and beautiful photogenic looks, Whitney was pursued by record company executives until Clive Davis, president of Arista Records signed her to a recording deal in April 1983. The two worked closely on a creative level, choosing the right material for her to record and the surest way of marketing her. Her self-named debut was released in March 1985, with "You Give Good Love" the first single. Both sold poorly initially until it was kick-started with the first of three extracted chart topping singles: "Saving All My Love For You", "How Will I Know" and "The Greatest Love Of All". The album topped the UK chart, a feat repeated across the world, and was nominated for four 1986 Grammy awards, but won only one for Best Pop Vocal Performance.

Whitney's life now hit the fast lane, she spent most of her time promoting her career. Said to be a millionaire at 22 years old, she had little private time and the media followed her every move and word. In 1986 Whitney headlined her first US tour, followed by concerts in the UK on her way through Europe. And, by the time her debut album had exceeded sales of 13 million globally, collecting multi-platinum albums and countless awards on the way, her second album was planned. Prior to the release of "Whitney", the extracted dance track "I Wanna Dance With Somebody (Who Loves Me)" shot to the top of the UK chart, a pattern repeated across the world. When the album was released, it entered the chart at the top; likewise globally. A pair of further singles followed – the ballad "Didn't We Almost Have It All?" and the uptempo "So Emotional", which marked Whitney's sixth consecutive US number one single. It was reported that she was now worth $44 million but still did not have a steady boyfriend so rumourmongers were out in force. However, that was to change. Meantime, her career continued to rise, she was the talk of the US, and the most sought after artist in the world.

In 1988 "Where Do Broken Hearts Go?" returned her to the top of the US chart and the UK top twenty. In June she returned to the UK to headline a concert at Wembley Stadium celebrating the 70th birthday of Nelson Mandela. The single "Love Will Save The Day" was issued to coincide with the visit, followed by her next UK chart topper "One Moment In Time". Next came her third album signalling a harder dance-orientated sound "I'm Your Baby Tonight" from which the title track was lifted as a single to top the US Hot 100 and UK top five.

During 1991, after enjoying her ninth US number one single with 'trademark' ballad "All The Man I Need" she returned to the UK for concerts at Wembley Arena and guested at an AIDS charity gala staged in London's Hyde Park. After years of being alone, Whitney announced her engagement to Hip-Hop/R&B artist Bobby Brown in May 1992 (they married in July) before starting filming "The Bodyguard".

Her acting debut as the stalked singer Rachel Marron in this romantic thriller/drama film alongside Kevin Costner impressed enough to ensure that Houston could comfortably become a successful duel singer/film actress in the vein of Cher/Diana Ross/Barbra Streisand, though her private life at this time onwards was portrayed as being shambolic to the say the least.

Incidentally the blueprint for the film dates back to the early 1980s and was to originally star Diana Ross in the Houston role though when the role was re-cast almost a decade later Madonna was considered before it was honoured as a suitable film debut for Houston five years after Arista Records signed a two year development deal with Tri-Star Pictures for her to move into films.

As well as the international chart topper "I Will Always Love You", the film also produced four further hits for Whitney over the next year – a cover of "I'm Every Woman", cloned ballads "I Have Nothing", "Run To You" and the upbeat "Queen Of The Night".

It's fair to say that The Bodyguard film/soundtrack turned around Houston's career.

At the 1994 NAACP Image Awards, the promo video for I'm Every Woman won Outstanding Music Video while Houston herself won Outstanding Female Artist & Entertainer Of the Year accolades at the same ceremony. Whilst at the 21st American Music Awards either Houston or the soundtrack album dominated the awards including those for Favourite Pop/Rock Female Artist, Pop/Rock Single (I Will Always Love You), Favourite Pop/Rock Album, Soul/R&B Female Artist, Soul/R&B Single (I Will Always Love You) and Adult Contemporary Album.

Her next film role, for which reportedly she commanded $10 million, was as Julia in "The Preacher's Wife" co-starring Denzel Washington. "I Believe In You And Me" was later lifted as a single. In March 1993 Whitney and Bobby became parents with the birth of their daughter Bobbi Kristina. Very soon it was a marriage destined for disaster, with drug abuse, and escalating financial problems, Whitney and her husband separated.

Late in 1995 her "Exhale (Shoop Shoop)" single, form the "Waiting To Exhale" film soundtrack was released as a top twenty UK hit, while the next year two singles hit the UK top twenty, namely, "Count On Me" a duet with CeCe Winnans, and "Step By Step". In 1998 she charted once with the Mariah Carey duet "When You Believe" taken from "The Prince Of Egypt" film soundtrack. Her career continued to yo-yo chartwise through to the next decade but rumours of her drug use which led to her unreliability ran rife throughout the industry. Her marriage to Bobby was reconciled, but it did not last, and they were finally divorced during 2006. The performances she did honour were sloppy and more often than not, she forgot her lyrics. When pictures of a rejuvenated Whitney later started to circulate the press, her diehard fans breathed easier. And with the solid encouragement of her mentor/friend Clive Davis, she finally released that long awaited comeback album during 2009 – "I Look To You". She was rewarded with the fastest selling female solo album to date. Then in 2011 she announced she was to star in "Sparkle" alongside Mike Epps and Jordin Sparks.

On 9 February 2012 after rehearsals for Clive Davis' pre-Grammy awards party, Whitney Houston made her last public performance with Kelly Price in Hollywood. On 11 February, she drowned in her bath in her Beverley Hilton Hotel room. She had been a long time user of drugs.

It was a tragic ending for one of America's iconic singers with a voice more befitting angels. Her legacy as one of the world's greatest performers will never be forgotten.

1993

MR BLOBBY/
MR BLOBBY'S THEME
MR BLOBBY

Harmless fun or just plain tomfoolery summed up this year's Christmas no.1. Mr Blobby evolved from Noel Edmonds House Party show which was a popular Saturday night light entertainment show in the mid-1990s. The programme was set in a village called Crinkley Bottom, and Mr Blobby first appeared in its second series, either in short sketches of lunacy or as an irritant to guest stars.

Actor Barry Killerby was the man behind the bow tied, yellow spotted pink foam costumed buffoon, who caused mayhem when he tumbled, or knocked down unsuspecting celebrities. The public, especially children, couldn't get enough of him, which led to a huge marketing campaign of spin-off books, toys, games - and eventually the obligatory single. Written and produced by Paul Shaw and David Rogers, the novelty self titled song was released by Destiny Music in December 1993, with hopes of clinching the Christmas top spot. It did, but Take That with their sentimental ballad "Babe" replaced it for one week, allowing Mr Blobby's irritating single to return.

The toothy grinning Mr Blobby - whose catchphrase was 'blobby, blobby, blobby', was never going to be a long time project, but the powers that be at Lancashire County Council paid Noel Edmonds's Unique company for the rights for a Morecombe-located theme park based around Crinkley Bottom village for £1 million. With hopes of making it a tourist attraction in future years, the theme park opened during the summer of 1994 and lasted three months, with the Council getting an earbashing from its auditors.

Let's face it, Mr Blobby's pop career would never run the same course as other fictitious creatures like The Muppets, Wombles, or Roland Rat, but he struggled on with one final release with 1995's "Christmas In Blobbyland" in the hopes of repeating his Festive success. The song reached the top forty and that was it. Then in 2005, Mr Blobby was seen briefly in Peter Kay's video of his charity single "Is This The Way To Amarillo", and since then has popped up on television programmes including an Eastenders skit on Harry Hills TV Burp. The Mr Blobby name was also used by John McLagan in the 1995 by-election for Littleborough & Saddleworth, and in 2012 appeared on the Big Fat Quiz Of The 90s.

One of the most irritating, yet successful, television characters was no more. It's now very hard to believe that a man inside a huge pink rubber costume covered with yellow blobs was so popular!

UK CHRISTMAS NUMBER ONES 1952-2022

1994

STAY ANOTHER DAY/ STAY ANOTHER DAY (3 MIXES)
EAST 17

The meteoric rise of young, good looking male vocal/dancing acts reached its peak in the mid 1990s. The so-named 'boy band' phenomenon included polished American imports like K7, EYC, Boyz II Men and Shai, while Worlds Apart, Bad Boys Inc and MN8 were flying the British flag in this genre, alongside two of the biggest groups of this period Take That and East East 17. Although Take That failed to achieve a Christmas chart topper - narrowly missing it in 1993 - their rivals East 17 stepped up their game for the Christmas 1994 top spot. Take That were the happy, smiling, safe group, whereas East 17 were the opposite.

Hailing from the E17 postal district of Walthamstow, London, the original 1991 line up of this visually distinctive vocal/dancing group comprised songwriter Tony Mortimer (born 21 October 1970), Brian Harvey (born 8 August 1974) and John Hendy (born 26 March 1971). When a London Records A&R manager heard Tony Mortimer's compositions, he was told to form a group which fitted the vacancy the company was looking for. The trio named itself after Walthamstow's postcode E17, and signed to Tom Watkins management company. Watkins wanted to launch a boy band to rival Take That and believed he had found that in East 17. Other group members included Robbie Craig, Terry Coldwell and Blair Dreelan.

Armed with a London Records' recording deal, their hip-hop style visual image and US soul/funk inspired sound, their projected moody, rough edged, no nonsense image, pushed them miles apart from their nearest rival Take That.

East 17 first charted in 1992 with two singles - the top ten entrant "House Of Love", inspired by the first Gulf War, and "Gold" which peaked in the top thirty. Their debut album "Walthamstow" followed a year later to hit the top spot. Their British success spread across Europe and beyond, earning them hit singles in numerous countries including Australia where they held the number one position with "It's Alright" for seven weeks in the singles chart. Without a doubt, 1993/1994 were the group's dominating years, when they were rarely out of the chart. For example, "Deep" hit the top five, followed by two top twenty hits – "It's Alright" and "West End Girls", a cover of The Pet Shop Boys' original. "Around The World", "Steam", featured in the 1998 film "Up 'N Under", and the Christmas number one during 1994.

UK CHRISTMAS NUMBER ONES 1952-2022

Following the release of their second album "Steam", "Stay Another Day" not strictly a Christmas themed song, was issued to catch the lucrative festive market. The song was a lush harmonic ballad inspired by personal tragedy, and written by Tony Mortimer, with Rob Keane and Dominic Hawken, who wrote the majority of East 17's material. "Stay Another Day" dominated the UK chart for five weeks and was their only chart topper. The promotional video obviously played an integral part in the single's longevity – Tony Mortimer played the piano while the group members were dressed in snow coats and boots, with fake snow all around them.

"Stay Another Day" was their biggest ever hit, but red lights were flashing dangerously because Brian Harvey felt the band were getting 'too pop'. He wanted to embrace their R&B influences more strongly. The result was "Hold My Body Tight" which narrowly missed the top ten in 1995, while teaming with British songstress Gabrielle, to revive Shai's US chart topper "If You Ever" to peak at number two in the Christmas 1996 chart. Following this success, Brian Harvey made an ill-advised remark on the drug Ecstasy which was linked to school girl Leah Betts' death from MDMA during 1995. A media uproar ensued, the matter was discussed in the House of Commons, the group's reputation was crushed. Brian Harvey was sacked immediately, and within months Tony Mortimer left the line-up claiming artistic clashes with the remaining members as the cause.

In 1998 Brian Harvey was reinstated by Terry Coldwell and John Hendy, which led to them being dropped by Tom Watkins management and London Records. Against all odds the band, without Tony Mortimer, briefly returned in late 1998 as E-17, with new management, new image and a recording deal with compilation specialists Telstar Records. This resulted with a pair of hits "Each Time" and "Betcha Can't Wait" at number two, both singles returning the act to their beloved R&B influences. Their "Resurrection" album failed to hit the top forty, which heralded the start of their demise without Tony Mortimer's input as composer. Subsequently, E-17 was dropped by Telstar Records in 1999, and the group disbanded.

However, "Stay Another Day" was set to return eight years later as a Christmas hit, when it was the flipside to Girls Aloud's "Sound Of The Underground" single.

With the sudden interest in 1990s music acts, spurred on by the surprise yet successful comeback of heyday rivals Take That in 2006, it came as no surprise when the original members of East 17 reunited for a comeback tour. After the one performance at London's Shepherd's Bush Empire in May 2006, John Hendy was unable to commit to further concerts due to his roofing business. The remaining line-up continued as a trio to play at low key venues until 2009 when they performed at the Glastonbury Festival, and later in the year, all four members played together at a charity organised to support the Born Free Foundation. Once again, the band dissolved. A year later another comeback tour was announced and in 2011 Blair Dreelan replaced Brian Harvey, only to leave again. Despite all the changes to the group membership, East 17 released their 5th studio album "Dark Light" in 2012 from which "I Can't Get You Off My Mind" was extracted as a single, and at time of writing,

John Hendy and Terry Coldwell are the only original East 17 members in a group that's still touring, though this time London soul singer Robbie Craig joined the line up.

During their prime, East 17 sold in excess of 18 million records worldwide, and for a while was one of the UK's most successful boy bands.

UK CHRISTMAS NUMBER ONES 1952-2022

1995

EARTH SONG/ EARTH SONG/ YOU ARE NOT ALONE
MICHAEL JACKSON

Selling 1.16 million copies by 2012, "Earth Song" entered the UK chart at the top where it stayed for six weeks, preventing "Free As A Bird", The Beatles' first single in 25 years from getting there! A controversial song by any standards, but the self-proclaimed "King Of Pop" was back where he belonged.

Michael Joseph Jackson was born in Gary, Indiana, on August 29th 1958 (died 25 June 2009). His parents Joe and Katharine went on to have seven sons in total – Sigmund (Jackie), Toriano Adaryll (Tito), Jermaine La Juane, Marlon David, Brandon (Marlon's twin died shortly after birth), Steven Randall (Randy) and three daughters Maureen (Rebbie), Latoya and Janet. Their father was guitarist with The Falcons, a Chicago-based blues group during the fifties, but he married young and started a family, leaving his music behind him. He transferred his interest in music to his family, and formed a family group. It's well publicised that young Michael did not enjoy the best of relationships with his father, publicly claiming he whipped him, verbally and mentally abused him. In the public eye, the young group was gaining popularity in their locality, and following the release of their first single "I'm A Big Boy Now" on Steeltown Records in 1968, the brothers joined Motown Records.

Now known as the Jackson 5, their debut "I Want You Back" single hit the top of the US chart, and most charts around the world. The title represented the first in a remarkable story and in a succession of million-selling singles and albums under the Motown banner, including "ABC", "The Love You Save", "I'll Be There", "Mama's Pearl" "Never Can Say Goodbye" among others. During the heady days of Jackson 5 mania, the world fell under their charm and talent. It was Beatle mania all over again. In time, the Jackson 5's cute lead singer, with the big afro and brightly coloured clothes, began to ascend from his brothers. His voice and his dance routines befitted a singer much older, and to capture this growing talent, Michael recorded his first solo single, the easy listening styled "Got To Be There". It was a global hit, and heralded the start of a new and remarkable career for the young singer of pop-soul. During his stay at Motown Michael continued to record with his brothers, but it was clear emphasis was placed on his solo status particularly when his "Ain't No Sunshine"- the Bill Withers's composition and "Ben", a song about his pet rat and the title song from the film of the same name. As Michael's career soared – he also remained a member of the Jackson 5 - the group suffered falling sales which led to animosity between them, resulting in the brothers, bar one (Jermaine) leaving Motown Records to sign to the CBS Records' Epic label. Jermaine Jackson remained at Motown to pursue a solo career and marry the company boss' daughter Hazel Gordy.

Under their new recording deal, Michael continued to record and perform with his brothers, now known as The Jacksons (as Motown owned the name Jackson 5), but Michael's star was about to rise as a soloist with the release of his 1979 "Off The Wall" album with "Don't Stop 'Til You Get Enough" as its first single. The album went on to sell in excess of ten million copies, its sales elevated by its title track released as a single, followed by "Rock With You", "She's Out Of My Life" and "Girlfriend". To cash in on his escalating selling power, Motown released "One Day In Your Life" from 1975. The remixed version released in 1981 hit the UK top spot, replacing Smokey Robinson's first solo UK chart topper "Being With You", the first time in Motown/UK's history that one company artist followed the other to the pole position.

Michael's next musical move was to narrate the story book for "ET – The Extra Terrestrial" for MCA Records in 1983. It was a total labour of love for Michael because, like so many, he cried and melted at the fate of the little alien creature depicted in Steven Spielberg's "ET" film. He also composed "Muscles" for Diana Ross, his one time guardian and mentor, and future inspiration. As big as "Off The Wall" was, Michael's next album reached unimaginable heights. "Thriller", released in December 1982, immediately topped the UK and US album charts, before spreading across the world. During its life, the album became the top selling album of all time, with sales reputed to be 61 million. It won a staggering eight Grammy Awards, and was the first to utilise promotional videos to their fullest extent, particularly for "Thriller" the single. It was a 13-minute adventure, directed by John Landis, where Michael co-starred with Ola Ray, "Playboy" centrefold model, as they mingled and danced with the undead who rose from their graves.

In this dark and eerie atmosphere, enter the zombies, of which Michael is one, for a ground breaking dance routine. Vincent Price's menacing, haunting laugh adds realism to this slice of horror which was the most influential pop music videos ever. It also marked him being asked to relinquish his membership of the Jehovah's Witness. Also during this period, Michael showed an interest in purchasing the remains of John Merrick, the Elephant Man, and to this end visited London's Medical College where he offered $1 million as his purchase price. His offer was declined. "Thriller", the album, had seven singles in all extracted, including "Billie Jean", "Beat It", "Wanna Be Starting Something" and "The Girl Is Mine" a duet with Paul McCartney. Following the release of "Billie Jean", Michael performed it on "Motown 25: Yesterday, Today, Forever", a gala celebrating the company's 25th anniversary. Joining Motown stars, past and present, as well as other guest performers like Jose Feliciano, Adam Ant and Linda Ronstadt, Michael performed with his brothers before performing a mimed version of "Billie Jean" where he debuted his moon dancing and wore his recent gimmick of a white glove.

The spin off from the public hysteria and fortune made with "Thriller", led to a reluctant Michael agreeing to tour again with his brothers. Pepsi Cola were keen to sponsor the project, and part of that sponsorship included the brothers endorsing the soft drink in a television commercial. During the filming before a live audience, a magnesium flash bomb ignited and set Michael's hair alight. He recovered at the burns department at Brotman Medical Centre, Culver City. To coincide with the tour, The Jacksons' "Victory" album was released in 1984, while Motown reissued his "Farewell My Summer Love" album. In 1985, Michael Jackson and Lionel Richie were inspired by the UK's Band Aid charity project that involved the release of the single "Do They Know It's Christmas", to write "We Are The World". They recruited some of America's finest musicians and singers to record the song under the name USA For Africa where proceeds were earmarked for the USA For Africa Fund.

Also around this time, Michael played the role of an intergalactic entertainer in the 17-minute, 3D "Captain EO" epic film for exclusive use by Disney's US entertainment parks, and was pictured walking in public wearing a surgical mask due to his obsession with hygiene. In June 1986 he had surgery on his face, was pictured in a hyperbaric chamber to extend his life, which was later revealed to be a sham. For some time it was apparent that Michael's skin colouring was growing lighter and lighter. Needless to say, media coverage was intensive, some reports claiming he actually bleached his skin. However, the more likely reason was him being diagnosed with vitiligo which could cause paler skin and an aversion to sunlight.

This in turn led to him applying pancake makeup to disguise the skin blotches. It also became apparent that Michael's face was changing: thinner nose and lips, wider eyes, more defined cheek bones, and a dimple created in his chin. He was also dropping weight. During his regular visits to his dermatologist, Michael met Debbie Rowe, his second wife and mother of his two eldest children – Prince (Michael Joseph Jackson) and Paris (Michael Katherine Jackson). When Debbie Rowe and Michael divorced in 1999, he had full custody of the children.

In 1987 "Bad" was released as the follow up to "Thriller", marking the last collaboration between Michael and producer Quincy Jones. The album's first single "I Just Can't Stop Loving You", a duet with the uncredited Siedah Garrett, began a further run of hit singles that included "The Way You Make Me Feel", "Man In The Mirror", "Dirty Diana", "Get It", a duet with Stevie Wonder, and the album's title. Within a week of the album's release, Michael headed out on world tour which reputedly grossed $125 million through its 15-country journey. His stage gimmick this time was wearing sticking plasters on three of his fingers. The show hit London in July 1988 where he performed seven concerts at Wembley Arena. Prior to one of the performances, Michael presented a cheque for £300,000 to Prince Charles and Princess Diana as a donation to The Prince's Trust. Early in 1989, his "Moonwalker" video was released which spanned his career to date. It grossed $30 million.

During 1989 Michael Jackson was a recluse, yet he was never far from the headlines as trumped up stories about him never failed to amaze. So much so, the British press nicknamed him 'Wacko Jacko" In 1990, President Bush proclaimed him as Entertainer of the Year before selected members of the public and media. A short time later, Michael was rushed to hospital after collapsing at home following a strenuous dance routine, and his recording contract with CBS, now known as Sony Records, was renegotiated to release his next album "Dangerous". "Black And White" was the first track lifted for single release, and during the accompanying promotional video, Michael was publicly criticised for constantly grabbing his crotch. Both single and album topped the world's charts. Once again he toured the world, and opened his Heal The World Foundation, to benefit international children's charities and ecology projects. Other lifted hits included "Remember The Time", "In The Closet" with 'cloaked' vocals by Princess Stephanie of Monaco, "Who Is It", "Jam", "Heal The World", "Give In To Me", featuring Slash, and "Will You Be There" from the 1993 film "Free Willy". Also in 1993 Jackson allowed himself to be interviewed by US talk show host Oprah Winfrey at his Neverland Ranch, in Santa Barbara County, California, which he purchased in 1988 as his home and his private amusement park. This was his first televised interview in almost 14 years.

The programme was both successful and problematic, and the latter would grow legs when his friendship with young Jordy Chandler hit the headlines. This resulted in Michael being reported to the Californian police authorities for child abuse – and the story hit the headlines. This prompted two of his former employees to confirm publicly that they had witnessed Michael molesting youngsters. While this nightmare was unfolding in America, Michael was abroad touring. Fearful that he would be arrested if he returned home, he was diverted to London to enter the Charter Nightingale Clinic to treat his growing dependency on pain killing medication.

Upon his later return to his Neverland Ranch, in December 1993, two policemen, a doctor and photographer visited Michael to photograph his genitalia and to examine him. Two days later, he appeared in a four-minute broadcast declaring his innocence to all charges against him. A year later, Michael and Jordy Chandler reached a financial settlement. While the public remained stunned at these allegations, Michael added to the disbelief by marrying Elvis Presley's only daughter Lisa Marie in May 1994. And as the year closed, all child abuse allegations against Michael were dropped.

In 1995, Jackson agreed to his music being repacked under the title "HIStory: Past, Present And Future". The release included several new tracks like his duet with sister Janet titled "Scream", "You Are Not Alone", and of course, his 1995 Christmas chart topper "Earth Song" which was his most successful UK single, selling in excess of one million copies. Intended for "Dangerous" and originally titled "What About Us", the ballad dealt with animal welfare and the rapidly declining environment, further establishing Michael as a socially conscious spokesman. The accompanying promotional film was particularly harrowing but no-one was left in any doubt of the message behind the music. Among the awards the song attracted was the Doris Day Music Award, given annually to those involved in high profiling or working towards animal issues.

In 1996 Michael performed "Earth Song" at the BRITS Awards ceremony in London where he had received the honour of Artist Of A Generation.

Following his performance of the song, Pulp frontman Jarvis Cocker ran to the stage, shoved his bum frontside and gave the V sign. He found the act offensive because Jackson had depicted himself as Jesus at his crucifixion, with movements indicating the power to heal the many children on stage with him.

The follow-up single to "Earth Song" was equally as potent in subject matter. "They Don't Care About Us", dealing with race relations was the album's fourth single, contained (unintentional) anti-Semitic lyrics and was one of his most controversial singles to date. Once again, Michael toured the world to support the release of "HIStory". In February 1998 he released a new video "Ghosts", a 40-minute blend of drama and dance that included the songs "Ghost", "2 Bad" and "Is It Scary?", the latter from his "Blood On The Dancefloor" CD.

Michael's next album "Invincible" was released in October 2001, his first full length studio album in six years, and his last while he lived. Due to lack or promotion, the album failed to reach the sales power of his previous releases, selling 13 million copies globally. A trio of singles were extracted, namely, "You Rock My World", "Cry" and "Butterflies". A year later, Michael won his 22nd American Music Award for Artist Of The Century, and his third child Blanket (Prince Michael Jackson II) was born. The mother's identity was unknown. It was Blanket that Michael dangled over the balcony of his fourth floor hotel room in Berlin, causing international media criticism.

Also in 2002 Michael gave freedom to TV personality Martin Bashir and his film crew for a UK documentary "Living With Michael Jackson", where during an interview Michael was seen holding hands with a young boy, Gavin Arvizo. Following the documentary's screening a year later, the Santa Barbara county attorney's office started a criminal investigation following complaints from Gavin Arvizo's mother of Michael's inappropriate behaviour with her son. In November 2003 Jackson was arrested, charged with seven counts of child molestation and two counts of giving Gavin an intoxicating agent. In June 2005, Michael was acquitted on all counts.

In 2006 the mansion at Neverland Ranch was closed as Michael's debts began spiralling at an alarming rate. He began working with composer/producer will.i.am but by 2007 the album still remained incomplete. To bridge the gap "Thriller 25" was released to mark the 25th anniversary of the original album, and in anticipation of Michael's 50th birthday, a series of greatest hits albums were released under the title "King Of Pop".

In March 2009 Michael held a press conference at London's O2 Arena to announce his intended to return to the performing stage with a series of "This Is It" concerts, his first major tour since 1997. It was to be his final curtain call and would raise the finances needed to pay off his numerous debtors. He intended to perform 50 concerts in London starting on 13 July 2009. Over one million tickets were sold in two hours, and within three weeks the concerts were sold out.

On 25 June 2009 Michael Jackson was found dead in his bedroom at 100 North Carolwood Drive, Holmby Hills, Los Angeles. His personal physician Conrad

Murray attempted to resuscitate him, but failed. CPR was administered by attending Los Angeles Fire Department paramedics, and resuscitation continued on the way to the Ronald Reagan UCLA Medical Centre. He was pronounced dead on arrival. Conrad Murray was later convicted of involuntary manslaughter. Shock and sadness spread across the world, and in the same way as Elvis Presley, John Lennon and Freddie Mercury before him, the public grief and demand was exploited by the record companies who held the rights to his recordings, resulting in the global charts being dominated by his singles and albums. Shortly after his death, over 50 of his recordings entered the British Top 200, with the re-issued "Man In The Mirror" heading the list to peak at number two. Without doubt Michael Jackson would continue to figure as a selling artist thanks to posthumous releases like "Michael", "Immortal" and "Xscape".

Unfounded allegations aside, Michael Jackson, like Elvis Presley before him, will continue to be newsworthy beyond the grave, and like him, and the legendary singers who inspired him, there will never be another Michael Jackson, regardless of the numerous imitation acts and soundalikes. Factually, Michael Jackson's contributions to the entertainment business are legendary. He was a global figure as he defined popular music, dance and vision, as well as being a foremost singer, composer and actor. He was the first artist to break down and expand musical barriers and is one of the most recognised artists on song and stage.

1996

2 BECOME 1/ SLEIGH RIDE
SPICE GIRLS

Without doubt the best selling singles act in the UK for 1996 were five young women who were initially known as 'Touch' but were renamed 'Spice' then the Spice Girls. The seeds had been planted via a journey that spanned Leeds, Liverpool and south east England and were finally sown in a house in Maidenhead! Yes, 'girl power' had truly arrived in a way that could not have been envisaged!

The original group was formed in 1994 by the family management team of Bob and Chris Herbert and Lindsey Casbon, who placed an advertisement in The Stage newspaper. Their intention was to give the chart-dominating boy bands like Take That a run for their money. Hoards of eager young girls flocked to audition at the Dance Works Studio in London for a much coveted place in this yet unnamed band. Eventually, after several auditions over a series of months, the numbers were slimmed to five, who were to spend months rehearsing in a house based in Boyn Hill Road, Maidenhead, Berkshire, where they were subsidised by Heart Management.

From there, the girls worked on demo recordings at South Hill Park Recording Studios in Bracknell, with studio owner/producer Michael Sparkes and composer Tim Hawes. One track "Sugar And Spice" sparked their final professional name. Before the final line-up was publicised, a further membership change took place, until five committed young women dedicated their lives to becoming pop singers – Emma Lee Bunton born on 21 January 1976 in Finchley, London; Geraldine Estelle 'Geri' Halliwell born 6 August 1972 in Watford, Hertfordshire, Melanie Jayne Chisholm born 12 January 1974 in Whiston, Merseyside, Victoria Caroline Adams born 17 April 1974 in Harlow, Essex, and Melanie Janine Brown born 29 May 1975 in Leeds, West Yorkshire.

Incidentally, Hertfordshire-based Michelle Stephenson a future TV reporter/presenter was in the prototype line-up but realised her heart wasn't in the project and she left to make way for Bunton a trained actress - the definitive line-up was found.

With rehearsals and recording continuing, the girls personally bonded, grew stronger, and wrote their first song together, "It's Just One Of Those Days". Using the name Touch, a showcase at the Trinity Studios for music business representatives was arranged, followed by another several months later when they debuted as Spice. As nothing concrete emerged from these showcases, the girls became increasingly concerned that they weren't being properly promoted or legally represented by their management team. With an armful of demo recordings and rehearsed choreography, the girls toured management agencies before devising a further showcase in Shepherds Bush before music industry A&R managers.

This time, the response was gratifying, with career promises made. Realising the pace was quickening, their management team created a legal contract to represent the group, but it was too late, the girls had other, more positive ideas which led to them meeting entrepreneur Simon Fuller. After working for Chrysalis Records, Fuller opened his own company 19 Entertainment, named after Paul Hardcastle's international hit "19", and, turning their back on their previous managers, the girls signed with him in March 1995. Within six months, after hawking demo singles and performance plans around major record companies like Polygram, Arista, Jive and EMI, a deal with Virgin Records was on the table.

With the legalities completed, a single was pencilled in for release, but before any decisions were made, the all-female group needed a gimmick. The idea of nicknames was hit upon, so the Spices were born. Geri Halliwell became 'Ginger Spice', as she had flame-coloured hair; Melanie Chisolm (Mel C) - 'Sporty Spice' due to her obvious fascination with fitness; Victoria Adams - 'Posh Spice', because she was extremely ladylike; Melanie Brown (Mel B) - 'Scary Spice' thanks to her wild and feisty personality, while Emma Bunton became 'Baby Spice', being the youngest of them all. The girls continued to gel, and their writing skills expanded as they wrote tracks with their debut album in mind.

But first things first. In July 1996, their first single, the bold, brash "Wannabe" was issued, accompanied by a ground breaking video. The hard work had paid off and to a certain extent the hype had worked. The single entered the UK chart at number three then shot to the top, where it stayed for seven weeks. It was also (at the time) the highest ever debut by a non-American group – beating The Beatles' "I Want To Hold Your Hand" - to hit the pole position where it stayed for four weeks. "Wannabe" went on to become a huge world hit, was the biggest selling debut single by a female group, and went on to become the biggest selling single by a female group of all time. A media frenzy grew out of proportion as the girls' every move was reported on; their faces graced teenage magazines and tabloid articles – everyone wanted a slice of this new musical discovery.

"Wannabe" was followed by the smooth, sweet swingbeat tinged "Say You'll Be There", another UK chart topper, this time for two weeks. Spice Girl-mania was taking over, and this led to being honoured by the industry. They won two BRIT awards - Best Video: "Say You'll Be There", and Best Single: "Wannabe" – and when the girls performed at the ceremony, Ginger Spice wore her famous Union Jack mini dress. Such was the storm it kicked up that it's now one of music history's most notorious outfits.

In November 1996, the debut album "Spice" was issued to hit the top spots on a global basis. It became the top selling album of the year, the biggest selling album by an all-female group, selling in excess of 28 million copies across the world with 1.8 million in the UK alone. A month later, the Spice Girls attracted over 500,000 people when they switched on the Christmas lights in Oxford Street, London.

Meanwhile, the race was hotting up for the top 1996 Christmas single. With a song written by the girls with composing/production duo Richard Stannard and Matt Rowe, the style was startlingly different from their first two releases. Backed with a version of 'Sleigh Ride', the top side , '2 Become 1', was a love song, where each Spice Girl sang a solo spot, reminiscent of The Three Degrees' style of ballad. It remains a mystery how the intimate/risqué nature of the lyrics bypassed the media censors; nevertheless the visually distinctive vocal quintet, with their 'girl power' slogan, racked their third British number one single and first at Christmas time.

Within a year the Spice Girls were the media darlings becoming the unofficial role models for impressionable young girls. Not content with this new sudden rush of fame, both in the UK and abroad, they were quickly signed up by firms to endorse products ranging from Walkers Crisps and Cadbury's to Pepsi. The Spice Girls' story was only just beginning and there was certainly going to be no stopping them!

(See also Christmas 1997 and 1998)

1997

TOO MUCH/ OUTA SPACE GIRLS/ TOO MUCH
SPICE GIRLS

The hottest female recording stars of the late 1990s were not newcomers Britney Spears or Christina Aguilera, or one hit wonders like Meredith Brooks or Jennifer Paige, but British quartet The Spice Girls. The feisty ladies took no prisoners as their grip on the world charts was tightened.

The first single of 1997 was the double headed "Mama"/"Who Do You Think You Are", the final track from the "Spice" album, and released to benefit Comic Relief. Once again, the single shot to the top, and by doing so the Spice Girls became the most successful debut act of all time – beating Gerry and the Pacemakers, Frankie Goes To Hollywood, Jive Bunny And The Mastermixes and Robson and Jerome, who all topped the chart with their first three singles. The Spice Girls extended that achievement to six, a figure beaten by Westlife in 2000.

From music to the written word, when the girls published their first book "Girl Power!", selling 200,000 copies in one day, later being translated into 20 languages. This was followed by "Spice: The Official Video Volume One", selling half a million units, and the announcement at the Cannes Film Festival that the group were to star in their own film titled "Spice World". In a year that was overflowing with honours and awards, the Spice Girls released their fifth single "Spice Up Your Life" from the film, which hit the top during October 1997. This same month, they performed for the first time in Istanbul, Turkey, before meeting Nelson Mandela in South Africa. In November, their second album "Spiceworld" was issued which set a new record for the fastest selling album by shipping seven million copies during its first two weeks on release. The album went on to sell over 20 million copies internationally.

Also during November, following their performance of "Spice Up your Life" on the MTV Europe Music Awards, they decided to fire their manager Simon Fuller to take care of themselves. The action was criticised by the media because Fuller was the mastermind behind the Spice Girls – which may or may not be true – but it's ironic (or coincidence) that their seventh single failed to hit the top.

"Spiceworld" featured guest slots from Elton John, Roger Moore and Meat Loaf, and was thought to be the 1990s' equivalent of The Beatles' 'A Hard Day's Night' - with five women not four men. As expected, the film's premiere was dominated by their fan base, which like The Beatles' fans, were predominately young excitable females. The song featured on the film's opening credits became the UK Christmas number one for 1997. Titled 'Too Much', it was inspired by the lounge ballad style of American singers like Nancy Wilson, Peggy Lee and Salena Jones; and it was perfect for the Christmas period.

Produced by the Absolute composing/production duo (Andy Watkins and Paul Wilson) and co-written by the Spice Girls, this swaying torch number dominated the top spot for two weeks, replaced by 'rival' group, All Saints with 'Never Ever'! This unit was considered to be a much cooler alternative to the Spice Girls, and as other all-female British acts, like Vanilla, N-Tyce and Honeyz, started to make their presence felt during the late 1990s, none, at this time, proved a serious threat to The Spice Girls.

Although 'Too Much' wasn't their final British chart topper, it seemed the girls were losing their impetus; that as quickly as they had risen, they were in danger of falling. Much of this, at the time, was placed on over-exposure because let's admit it, there are only so many times you can say or hear the words 'girl power'. That point was proven when the sixties soul style sound of their 'Stop' single peaked at number two early in 1998. Added to this, the group splintered when Geri Halliwell decided to quit for a solo career, while Mel B and Victoria Adams announced they were pregnant. The final song to feature all five members was the lightweight 'Viva Forever' which restored them to the top spot during August 1998, and perhaps helped by its touching animated promotional video.

Prior to Geri's departure, said to be influenced by exhaustion and disharmony with other group members, the Spice Girls toured the world early in 1998, before returning to the UK to perform a pair of sell out concerts at London's Wembley Arena, followed by twelve dates at Birmingham's NEC Arena. The concerts were recorded for a live album later in the year, but it failed to materialise. They were then invited to sing alongside numerous 'Indie' musicians such as Ian McCulloch of Echo and The Bunnymen who penned the track, Simon Fowler of Ocean Colour Scene and Tommy Scott of Space on the official England World Cup song under the banner of 'England United' and titled "How Does It Feel (To Be Top Of The World)". Though football fans much preferred the re-release of the Lightning Seeds' anthem "Three Lions".

The new slimmed down Spice Girls were determined the group would continue, but with Geri's departure recorded material had to be scrapped, and contracts signed had to be voided. It was a messy legal business, with the media hanging on to every word. Yet, the quartet rode the wave to enjoy further success.

(See also Christmas 1996 and 1998)

UK CHRISTMAS NUMBER ONES 1952-2022

1998

GOODBYE/ CHRISTMAS WRAPPING/ GOODBYE ORCHESTRAL
SPICE GIRLS

Within two short years The Spice Girls became bait for the media with 'kiss and tell' tales and ill-advised quotes well publicised. The girls were fair game, but on the music front they held their heads up high by scoring their third and final consecutive Christmas no 1 single.

With the distinction that they were the first UK female group to ever achieve this feat, the song 'Goodbye' which was written by all five Spice Girls with their producers Richard Stannard and Matt Rowe during an American tour, featured all but one of the original line-up. 'Ginger Spice' had left the group membership during mid-1998 for a solo career. It was initially intended to record the poignant song, a tribute to the departed Geri, in Nashville, but instead of the planned country music influence, it followed the same adult-orientated ballad vein as their two previous Christmas chart toppers.

In some ways the song showed the cracks in the group's relationship, with all five women gradually becoming individual superstars in their own right. Mel B/'Scary Spice' married Dutch dancer Jimmy Gulzar and became known as Mel G. She gave birth to Phoenix Chi during February 1999 and was also the first Spice Girl to score a solo number one single with 'I Want You Back' in September 1998. Recorded under the name Melanie B, it was included in the soundtrack of the film "Why Do Fools Fall In Love", and also appeared on her solo "Hot" album. After announcing her engagement to superstar footballer David Beckham in 1998, the couple quickly dubbed 'Posh and Becks' by the media. In July 1999 expectant mother, Victoria Adams/'Posh Spice' married her footballer, attracting huge international attention.

Meanwhile, Emma Bunton/'Baby Spice' was groomed by Virgin Records for a solo career, initially teaming her up with alternative dance act Tin Tin Out in 1999, before her first solo recording in a dance/pop vein with 2001's "A Girl Like Me". However, she really took off as a MOR style vocal act when signed to a 'third party' deal with 19 Management's label offshoot 19 Records and via Universal Records released two studio albums - 2003's "Free Me" and "Life In Mono" three years later. She then switched to television and radio work. Melanie Chisholm/'Sporty Spice' musically ditched pop, for a brash - yet cool - R&B/rock style (prototyping P!nk and Anastascia) on her way to become the

126

best selling solo Spice with two Virgin released albums, "Northern Star" in 1999 and "Reason" during 2003. Following her dismissal from Virgin Records, Melanie issued her 2005 comeback album "Beautiful Intentions" on her own Red Girl label, developing a superstar following outside the UK. She also became a first-time mother in 2009.

Geri Halliwell was quickly snapped up for a solo deal with EMI Records' subsidiary Chrysalis, and within a year of leaving her Ginger alter-ego behind, she quickly became known as a female 'Robbie Williams'. Scoring three hit singles including two number one titles "Mi Chico Latino" and "Lift Me up" in 1999; "Bag it Up" a year later, and her version of The Weather Girls' classic "It's Raining Men" in 2001, she had carved a new solo career for herself as a singer. This led to other entertainment projects elevating her into the British media superstar bracket. She also became a mum for the first time in 2006, and served the United Nations as a Goodwill Ambassador.

Back to 1998 and following their world tour which covered Europe and North America, and Geri's departure, the four remaining Spice Girls continued to record new material, and once again secured the UK pole position over Christmas. With their 1998 release "Goodbye" (originally earmarked for the "Spice World" project) the Spice Girls became the only second act, next to The Beatles, to hold the Festive number one position for three consecutive years. "Goodbye" was their fourth best selling single, and their eighth number one title in the UK.

It also signalled the end for the working partnership of the song's producers and co-writers Richard Stannard and Matt Rowe. The next year, The Spice Girls returned to the recording studio to begin work on their third album "Forever" from which "Holler"/"Let Love Lead The Way" was extracted as a single: another chart topping title. Within a year, the foursome fractured and, while insisting they weren't splitting up, each member was pursuing a solo career.

During their heyday the Spice Girls reputedly amassed a personal fortune of £20 million a piece, including their take from merchandise, personal appearances on top of record sales. And, singlehandedly they returned 'pure pop' to the fore as a serious and dominant music style. So, it really came as no surprise in 2007 when the Spice Girls announced they were to reform for concert and recording duties – and in their original hit line up! The "Return Of The Spice Girls" world tour started in Vancouver in December 2007, and when tickets sales went on sale in London, they sold out within 38 seconds with over one million fans signing up for them. It was estimated that five million fans bid for tickets across the world. Their comeback single "Headlines (Friendship Never Ends)" became the official Children In Need charity single for 2007.

In 2010 the Spice Girls won the BRIT award for Best Performance Of The 30th Year, a new category, and they, with Simon Fuller, teamed up with Jennifer Saunders and Judy Craymer to develop a musical "Viva Forever" which did not feature the actual group members, but their music.

It is almost 30 years since the Spice Girls were formed and burst onto the music scene with "Wannabe", and there are very few people who do not know their name or heard their music. Today, (2023) each member remains very much in the public eye. They were, without any doubt, the 'girl power' phenomenon of the 1990s, bringing with them a whole new sound and style of dress, and were the most recognised group since The Beatles.

(See also Christmas 1996 and Christmas 1997)

1999

I HAVE A DREAM/ SEASONS IN THE SUN
WESTLIFE

With the demise of Boyzone, and the waning interest in The Spice Girls, the teen market needed a new singular gender group- and that came with Westlife, from Irish descent, who were managed by Louis Walsh and signed, at one time, to Simon Cowell's Syco record label. They couldn't go wrong!

The original six piece group comprised Mark Feehily, Kian Egan, Shane Filan, Derrick Lacey, Graham Keighron and Michael Garrett. Known as Six To One, later IOYOU, they released the single "Together Girl Forever". Shane Filan's mother contacted Louis Walsh, manager of fellow Irish band Boyzone, for an audition but they failed to secure a deal with Simon Cowell at BMG Records. However, Cowell told them that if they shed three members who had the least talent, they stood a chance. Subsequently, Garrett, Keighron and Lacey were dropped, to be replaced by Brian McFadden and Nicky Byrne.

The line-up of the new group read as follows: Nicky Byrne, born on 9 October 1978 in Dublin, Bryan McFadden, born on 12 April 1980 also in Dublin, Sligo-born Shane Filan on 5 July 1979, Kian Egan on 29 April 1980, and Mark Feehily born 28 May 1980. They chose the name Westside but as this was already used by another group, changed it to Westlife. Boyzone member Ronan Keating managed the new group with Louis Walsh, and in 1998 they enjoyed their first big break by supporting Boyzone and Backstreet Boys on tour. A year later they released their first single "Swear It Again" which topped the UK chart in May 1999. This began the run of seven consecutive number one singles that included "Flying Without Wings" (included in the soundtrack of the movie "Pokemon:The Movie 2000"), "I Have A Dream"/"Seasons In The Sun", "Fool Again", "Against All Odds (Take A Look At Me Now)" with Mariah Carey, and "My Love".

Westlife was the first boy band to have their first two singles enter the chart at the top, and the first to secure seven consecutive chart toppers faster than any other act, including Elvis Presley.

"I Have A Dream"/"Seasons In The Wind" was released as a double A-sider to capture the Christmas market. The group broke away from original material to re-record two classics from the 1970s , namely, Abba's "I Have A Dream" (1979) and Terry Jacks' "Seasons In The Sun" (1974). It was an ideal Christmas song, bursting with melody and tight vocals, and was the last UK number one title of the decade and, of course, the century. Both songs were featured on their self titled debut album released in November 1999 which shot to no 2 in the chart, selling over five million copies worldwide.

Westlife continued to rely on the adult-orientated music format resulting in a total of (to date) 17 UK number one singles, that included cover versions and original material, fulfilling their public's demand. "Coast To Coast" earned the distinction of being the UK's fourth top selling album in 2000 and a year later they embarked upon their first world tour. A trio of chart toppers were extracted from the 2001 "World Of Our Own" album – "Uptown Girl" (released in aid of Comic Relief), "Queen Of My Heart" and "World Of Our Own". Two years later, following the release of their fourth studio album "Turnaround", Westlife's version of the Barry Manilow classic "Mandy" returned them to the UK pole position. It seemed they could do no wrong, but life was to change. Shortly before their fourth world tour, Brian McFadden left Westlife to concentrate on a solo career and to spend more time with his family. His last performance with them was in February 2004. McFadden wanted to record more rock slanted material, perhaps motivated by the style of their 2003 single "Hey Whatever" which resembled Bryan Adams' style of music.

Unfortunately, his solo career lasted less than a year and his solo contract with Sony Music was cancelled. Meanwhile, the remaining Westlife membership continued to work and in 2005 released their comeback single "You Raise Me up", extracted from their "Face To Face" album. Both single and album soared to the pole position in their respective charts. Towards the end of the year, they duetted with Diana Ross on her classic "When You Tell Me That You Love Me". It peaked at number two. "Amazing" followed, a number four hit, whereupon the group toured extensively across the world, performing in China for the first time.

Following a long-term deal with Sony BMG in 2006, Westlife released "The Love Album" which outsold other similar compilations at the time to hit the top spot. When their version of Bette Midler's "The Rose" was lifted as a single, that too went straight to number one. Regular tours and releases ensured the group stayed in the public eye, and by 2008 they were confirmed by the industry's trade magazine Music Week as the seventh top touring act of the year. To mark the tenth anniversary in music, the group embarked upon the "10 Years Of Westlife" world tour, following which they would take an overdue hiatus from the business. A year later, their "Where We Are" album provided a handful of singles including "Safe", their 25th top ten UK single. Also in 2011, Westlife announced a split from Syco Records.

They re-signed with RCA to release a "Greatest Hits" project which fuelled rumours of an imminent split. However, later in the year, a UK "Greatest Hits" tour was announced with date booked for May 2012, after which they would definitely disband. The tour sold out within minutes. Two performances were filmed by ITV to be screened as "Westlife: For The Last Time" and "The Westlife Show", while the "Greatest Hits" compilation peaked at number four in the UK.

The final Westlife concerts took place over two June days at the Croke Park Stadium, Dublin, and one performance was globally screened live across 200 cinemas in four continents. It seemed that from this moment onwards the quintet turned quartet were officially no more.

Meanwhile the former frontman Shane Filan was confirmed in early 2013 as signing as a solo artist, initially signed to London Records before moving over to Atlantic Records.

In 13 years, Westlife topped the UK singles chart 14 times, recorded ten studio albums and sold over 50 million albums worldwide. As of writing, Westlife are the 34th top selling UK singles act in the UK, but never successfully cracked the US.

2000

CAN WE FIX IT?/ BOB'S LINE DANCE/ CAN WE FIX IT? (KARAOKE)
BOB THE BUILDER

Thanks to the growing popularity of a British children's television favourite, it was inevitable that at some point a Christmas single would be released to cash in on the festive period. So this Christmas a builder dominated the singles' chart.

BBC TV broadcasted the Hot Animation/HIT Entertainment produced programme Bob The Builder which became a surprise across-the-board success with its silicone skinned, titanium skeleton like animations, that were known as Bob the Builder and his friends. Created by Keith Chapman, this animated children's show went on to become a global smash. Actor Neil Morrisey voiced the show's title character for the British broadcast, while in America that honour was given to Canadian actor, Greg Proops.

The tale of the obliging and optimistic, hard-hatted, tool draped builder and his friends who included JJ, Wendy and Farmer Pickles, was the runaway television hit of 1999 and, by 2000 the potential was certainly there for something more to happen. BBC Records perhaps sensing the potential of recording a single, approached composer Paul K Joyce - formerly of the band Sense - to write a theme that would be palatable for radio play and, more importantly, have selling power. Also voiced by Neil Morrisey, the end result was known for its repetitive lyrical reply of 'Yes We Can' to the song's title.

Dominating the Christmas/New Year cusp, and joking aside, "Bob The Builder" actually won an Ivor Novello award, and was the best selling single for 2000, shifting 188,000 copies in just a week! It went on to sell over one million copies to become the most successful single in the history of the BBC. Merchandising was also a natural spin off, with Bob the Builder games, characters, equipment, models and so on, and these items remain as popular today with young viewers as do the original television programmes.

Another Bob 'stronghold' was Australia where the single topped their chart early in 2001, while a cover version of Lou Bega's "Mambo No.5" was issued as the follow up for the UK, another number one title. Both singles were featured on 'The Album' which hit number five on the UK chart.

Bob the Builder was a global success. The television shows were screened in over thirty countries in a variety of languages. Let's face it, it is quite rare that a television 'personality' like Bob has longevity in the music business, but happily for his creators, the animated builder in the hard hat is still a part of a growing child's life.

UK CHRISTMAS NUMBER ONES 1952-2022

2001

SOMETHING STUPID/ LET'S FACE THE MUSIC AND DANCE/ THAT'S LIFE
ROBBIE WILLIAMS & NICOLE KIDMAN

Take one classic transatlantic number one single of the 1960s, originally performed by a superstar singer/entertainer father and his pop singing, pin-up daughter, which almost 35 years later found itself heading the UK Christmas 2001 singles chart, this time recorded by a young British pop superstar and a globally respected Australian actress. Yes, as unlikely as it sounds, that is exactly what happened. Although a love duet, "Something Stupid" was a massive hit title in 1967 for Frank and Nancy Sinatra, and in Christmas 2001 the song dominated the UK chart thanks to Robbie Williams and Nicole Kidman.

The story behind the hit dates back to 1967, when Frank Sinatra approached his daughter's producer Lee Hazlewood for suitable songs for him and Nancy to record as a duet. He chose C Carson Parks composition "Something Stupid", who recorded the original version with his wife Gaile Foote in 1966. Despite being a love song, he knew it would be a hit for them both; even their record company was concerned that a father and daughter should want to sing the song, but bowed down to Sinatra's insistence. All worries were dismissed when the single topped the international charts during the Spring 1967. Nonetheless, it was nicknamed "the incest song", a title that stuck.

Now, it was time for another version. Robbie Williams was born on 13 February 1974, in Stock-on-Trent, Staffordshire. While at school he joined drama groups where his most prestigious role was as the Artful Dodger in "Oliver!". In 1990, after replying to an advertisement, he joined Take That, as the group's youngest member at 16 years old. Comprising Gary Barlow, Howard Donald, Jason Orange, Mark Owen, Robbie was their 'odd ball'; always joking and an unashamed extrovert. This in time led to group tension. Feeling overshadowed by Gary Barlow (composer and lead singer), Robbie took to alcohol and drugs. By 1995 his intake was worryingly high, he became increasingly belligerent and his dedication to the group became practically non-existent. He eventually he left the line-up in 1995. Take That disbanded in February 1996, leaving behind them an array of hit singles - "Once You've Tasted Love", "It Only Takes A Minute Girl", "A Million Love Songs" and "Could It Be Magic".

Robbie Williams pursued a solo career, signed to Chrysalis Records, and enjoyed his first hit "Freedom" in 1996. A year later he had released the evergreen "Angels", followed by "Let Me Entertain You", his first solo chart topper "Millennium" and "No Regrets". A year later he was named Best British Male at the BRIT Awards ceremony, a title he won for the next three consecutive years. The hits continued through the late 1990s into the next decade – "She's The One", "Rock DJ", "Kids" (his duet with Kylie Minogue), "Supreme" and "Eternity". His high profile earned him the title of the UK's top solo male artist and this accolade was repeated across the world.

Nicole Kidman was born on 20 June 1967, in Hawaii, while her Australian parents were visiting America on educational visas. They returned to Australia when she was four years old, where later on she showed an aptitude for acting and dancing at school. As a teenager she studied mime, drama and performing, making her film debut at the age of 16, in the 1983 film "Bush Christmas". By the end of the year she had a supporting role in an Australian television series, and appeared in low budgeted films, earning public attention due to the risqué nature of some scenes. She enjoyed her movie breakthrough during 1989 in "Dead Calm", and went on to star in several high ranking films during the early 1990s, peaking in "Days Of Thunder", where she starred alongside Tom Cruise, her future husband. When that ended in divorce, Nicole married Australian country singer, Keith Urban. "Far And Away" and "Batman Forever" established her as a global actress of note. Other money spinning films followed – "To Die For", "Eyes Wide Shut", "Australia" and more recently "Grace Of Monaco".

Robbie Williams was inspired to contact Nicole Kidman after seeing her performance in the 2001 film "Moulin Rouge" where she starred opposite Ewan McGregor. Nicole played a courtesan, earned her a Golden Globe Award, and marked her debut as a duettist with McGregor singing "Come What May", released the same year to peak in the UK top thirty singles chart. The singer and actress met in Los Angeles to record their version of "Something Stupid" for inclusion on Robbie's "Swing When You're Winning" album which saw Williams break away from mainstream/pop music to record lounge/MOR material inspired by The Rat Pack and Bobby Darin.

The extracted single sold over 98,000 copies in the first week of release, elevating to 366,000 copies in all, earning it silver status. It was also the 30th top selling UK single of the year, and Robbie Williams' best selling top ten single across Europe.

In 2006 Take That reunited for a television documentary "Take That: For The Record", and that the next year they were going to tour, without Robbie. This led to a return to the recording studio from which their comeback album "Beautiful World" was issued. Extracted singles were all worldwide hits – "Shine", "Patience", "I'd Wait For Life". The group then hit the road again with their Beautiful World Tour 2007. "Greatest Day" was the first single to be lifted from their second album "The Circus" and as the hits poured in, Take That mania was in full throttle. After writing the single "Shame" with Gary Barlow, Robbie Williams returned to the group during 2010, and following the release of "The Flood" from the group's next album "Progress", the whole group embarked on a world tour. The project was an unprecedented success with huge financial rewards. In 2011 the Take That membership embarked upon individual projects. Robbie returned to his career, married actress Ayda Field and they since have had four children at time of writing.

It seems likely that Robbie Williams will continue as a soloist thanks to million selling albums like "Swing When You're Winning" in 2001, followed a year later by "Escapology". "Intensive Care" saw 2005 release, with "Rudebox" the next year. After signing with Universal Records he released the retrospective compilation "Consciousness:The Greatest Hits 1990 – 2010" which hit the top spot, whereupon his debut 'new' album "Take The Crown" was Robbie at his best. Another chart topping title. Likewise his 2013 album "Swings Both Ways".

To date, Robbie is the best selling British solo artist in the UK, has sold more than 75 million albums and singles worldwide, and has been honoured with 17 BRIT Awards. He was entered into the "Guinness Book Of World Records" for selling 1.6 million tickets in one day for his 2006 "Close Encounters Tour", and six of his albums are in the top 100 biggest selling chart in the UK. The accolades and honours are endless.

In mid -2016 it was announced that Robbie Williams signed a new record deal with Sony Music's Columbia Records imprint for his future solo recording commitments.

Robbie Williams has also achieved something Take That has failed to do (so far) – top the UK singles chart over the Christmas period! – He certainly has some staying power.

2002

SOUND OF THE UNDERGROUND/ STAY ANOTHER DAY/ SOUND OF THE UNDERGROUND (REMIX)
GIRLS ALOUD

The first half of the 2000s was saturated with reality television shows in the UK, with the most successful being either celebrity based, or associated with weekly music orientated talent shows like "Fame Academy" and "Pop Idol" offering unknown acts five minutes of fame or the winner's pot. However, it was during the 2002 show "Popstars:The Rivals" that the all-female vocal group Girls Aloud was formed, and within two weeks of their winning the show, their debut single was released to hit the Christmas top spot!

Girls Aloud comprised Cheryl Cole (nee Tweedy), born 30 June 1983 in Newcastle upon Tyne, Tyne and Wear; Nadine Coyle, born 15 June 1985, in Derry, Northern Ireland; Sarah Harding, born 17 November 1981, in Ascot, Berkshire; Nicola Roberts, born 5 October 1985, in Stamford, Lincolnshire, and Kimberley Walsh, born 20 November 1981, in Bradford, West Yorkshire. The girls won the viewing public's vote. Their hastily released song "Sound Of The Underground" and a version of East 17's "Stay Another Day", was intended for the little-known act Orchid, and Girls Aloud merely added their vocals over the existing song. The single dominated the UK chart for four weeks, passing platinum sales on the way, selling over 213,000 copies.

However, with success, came disaster. John McMahon, their road manager, was killed in a car accident, and Cheryl Cole was arrested for a vicious assault and alleged racist remarks aimed at a black female toilet attendant in a Surrey nightclub. She was found guilty and received a £3,000 fine and community service. The girls maintained a low profile as they spent five months in the studio recording their debut album. The "Sound Of The Underground" album was released during May 2003, entering the chart at number two. And another platinum seller. "No Good Advice" was extracted for single release to hit number two, followed by "Life Got Cold", a number three UK hit. A version of The Pointer Sisters' "Jump" also hit the top two.

A year later, the group's second album "What Will The Neighbours Say?" from which "The Show" was lifted. The single entered the chart at number two. Likewise their next, "Love Machine" which was followed by their version of The Pretenders' "I'll Stand By you", issued as the official Children In Need charity single. It hit the top although critics disliked it. As their second album passed platinum status, Girls Aloud announced details of their first tour "What Will The Neighbours Say? Live" starting in May 2005.

Once the tour was complete, the girls worked on their third album "Chemistry". Surprisingly, it failed to repeat previous successes by peaking in the top twenty, and when the first single "Long Hot Summer" was extracted it ended Girl Aloud's run of top five placings. "Biology" and "See The Day" were among other singles to be released from "Chemistry", but sales were declining.

Also in 2005, the girls filmed the documentary "Girls Aloud: Home Truths", and this success led to a six-part series. A year later, they embarked upon their first arena tour, and released the compilation "The Sound Of Girls Aloud: The Greatest Hits" which hit the chart at the top. Sales topped the one million mark. With the single "Something Kinda Ooooh", Girls Aloud were the first UK act to hit the top five on download sales only. Among their other releases in 2007, Girls Aloud teamed up with UK girl group Sugababes to record a version of Aerosmith's "Walk This Way" as the official single for Comic Relief. It marked their third chart topper.

From 2009 through to 2006 Girls Aloud continued their high profile as recording and touring artists. Singles from the "Tangled Up" and "Out Of Control" albums ensured regular chart placings. They played hostess for a second television series "The Passions Of Girls Aloud", and recorded a pair of songs for the soundtrack to the "St Trinian's" film. "Out Of Control" released during November 2008 was in fact, the girls' last studio album. It hit the chart at number one and was praised as their best album ever. "The Promise" track was extracted to top the UK chart, their fourth. Further singles were issued, supported by lengthy tours, until 2009 when they took a two/three year hiatus.

Girls Aloud reunited in 2012 for their 10th anniversary, releasing "Something New" as the official charity single for Children In Need. As that reached number two in the UK chart, their second greatest hits album "Ten" and "Beautiful 'Cause You Love Me" followed. In March 2013 the group performed their last concert together in Liverpool.

The individual group members pursued solo careers. Sarah Harding who became an actress and intended to pursue a solo singing career sadly passed away in 2021 after losing a battle with breast cancer , while Nadine Coyle released her debut album "Insatiable" in 2010 on her own Black Pen Records imprint. It reached the top fifty, as the album's title hit the singles top thirty. Nicola Roberts issued her "Cinderella's Eyes" album via A&M Records. A top twenty hit. Kimberley Walsh became a television presenter, made her West End debut in "Shrek: The Musical" and competed in "Strictly Come Dancing" before recording as a soloist. But the most newsworthy being Cheryl Cole who, apart from marrying and divorcing footballer Ashley Cole, became a bankable singer. She also joined Simon Cowell's ranks on "X Factor" for a time; left and returned again.

Girls Aloud are the most successful reality television group (at 2023), earning £30 million during their tenure as the UK's biggest selling girl group of the 21st century.

2003

MAD WORLD/ NO POETRY/ MAD WORLD (ALTERNATE VERSION)
MICHAEL ANDREWS FT GARY JULES

This Christmas chart was dominated by a two-year-old recording by an American singer/songwriter covering an 1980s electro-pop classic as a left field ballad.

"Mad World" was originally a UK top five hit in 1982 for the West Country duo Tears For Fears, and was covered by Michael Andrews and Gary Jules for the soundtrack to the film "Donnie Darko" in 2001. Penned by Roland Orzabal, the song was influenced by "The Primal Scream" written by Arthur Janon, and according to Orzabal was – "(throwing) together a lot of different images to paint a picture without saying anything specific about the world". Years after its conception, "Mad World" is an American television favourite and can be heard on programmes like "CSI: Crime Scene Investigation", "Without A Trace" and in the advertising for "Gears Of Fear" video game.

Gary Jules, born on 19 March 1969, in Fresno, California, was part of the contemporary cult American singer/songwriters who never quite 'made it', like Gregg Alexander, Van Hunt and Michelle Branch, although in fairness, his belated breakthrough lies with record company politics at the time. Having been a member of various bands in the Los Angeles area since the late 1980s, he found himself a decade later signed to an A&M Records solo contract, under which the badly timed "Greetings From The Side" album was issued. The label was being restructured at the time of the album's release, with internal mergers and acquisitions, subsequently "Greetings From The Side" was lost in the corporate shuffle. As a result Jules was dropped by A&M.

Undeterred, he was persuaded by Michael Andrews (born on 17 November 1967, in San Diego, California) a long time friend and the producer of his debut album, to record the song as it would be perfect for the closing credits of director Richard Kelly's movie.

A perfect fit!

Young director Kelly wanted an 1980s themed soundtrack for "Donnie Darko" and Gary Jules' ethereal rendition of the song suited the nature of the sensitive drama. Regrettably, the film's 2001 success was mediocre; it didn't become a hit until 2003 when, thanks to pressure from a growing cult following, the film was commercially released on DVD. This had a knock-on effect because the subsequent radio airplay of "Mad World" – credited to Michael Andrews featuring Gary Jules and released by Sanctuary Records - elevated it to the top of the UK Christmas chart, where it spent three weeks in total. The single was also the second consecutive UK chart topper for Sanctuary Records, following "Changes" by Ozzy and Kelly Osbourne.

Popular for his tweed flat cap, guitar and angelic voice - a cross between REM's Michael Stipe and Art Garfunkel - Gary Jules has (at the time of writing) joined the ever growing ranks of 'one hit wonders', although his 2001-recorded album "Trading Snakeoil For Wolftickets" was finally issued to cash in on the Christmas single's success. It peaked in the UK top forty chart. Two years later, Gary Jules recorded his third studio album, titled after his name.

2004

DO THEY KNOW IT'S CHRISTMAS?/ DO THEY KNOW IT'S CHRISTMAS?
BAND AID 20

Twenty years on from the definitive original, and 15 years after the second version, the time had come for a reworking of the Midge Ure and Bob Geldof song, following a suggestion by The Sun newspaper journalist Dominic Monahan. The song was recorded during November 2004 to help provide much needed funds for famine relief in Sudan's Darfur area. The single was the UK's top selling single of the year.

Alternative rock producer Nigel Godrich produced the backing track at George Martin's North London studio, upon which the following artists would put their vocals: Daniel and Natasha Bedingfield, Bono, Busted, Coldplay's Chris Martin, Dizzee Rascal, Ms Dynamite, Morcheeba's Skye Edwards, Estell, The Divine Comedy's Neil Hammon, The Darkness' Justin Hawkins, Jamelia, Keane's Tom Chaplin and Tim Rice-Oxley, Beverley Knight, Lemar, All Saints' Shaznay Lewis, Katie Melua, Miloko's Roisin Murphy, Feeder, Snow Patrol, Rachel Stevens, Joss Stone, Sugababes, The Thrills, and Turin Brakes, Will Young and Travis' Fran Healy. Robbie Williams performed from a Los Angeles studio, while Dido performed separately from a Melbourne studio. Paul McCartney played bass guitar, Thom Yorke – piano, The Darkness' Justin Hawkins and Dan Hawkins, Radiohead's Jonny Greenwood – guitar, and Supergrass' Danny Goffey – the drums.

Calling themselves Band Aid 20 allowed the original song to be updated into the 21st century, and a rap performed by the contributing Dizzee Rascal was included within the song. This version was issued by Mercury Records.

"Do They Know It's Christmas?" debuted simultaneously on BBC Radio 1's The Chris Moyles Show and at 8am on breakfast shows on Capital and Virgin Radio, while the promotional video, with Madonna on the introduction, was screened across the UK on numerous channels that included the five terrestrial ones at 5.55pm on 18 November, four days after the single was recorded. Following this, a documentary "Band Aid 20: Justice Not Charity" was screened on 6 December by BBC TV.

Within the first day of its release, "Do They Know It's Christmas?" sold more than 72,000 copies, elevating it directly to the top of the chart. Within the first week, the CD version topped the 200,000 sales figure, and following the resolution of a dispute with Apple Computer iTunes' Music Store which had a fixed-price policy, the song shot to number eight on the download chart. WebTV encouraged their customers to purchase the single and video on their mobile phones, while HMV entertainment shops, opened earlier to enable customers more time to purchase the CD. At Edinburgh's HMV shop, Prime Minister Tony Blair was pictured purchasing a copy. The media, corporate and public support was once again overwhelming.

With the revived single once again highlighting the plight of East Africans, millionaire businessman Tom Hunter was moved to double the amount of money raised. And to keep the project in the public eye, the international concert, "Live 8" was staged on 2 July 2005 in London's Hyde Park. An estimated three billion people watched the greatest show on earth, or (as hyped) "A Day That Rocked The World". Artists like Annie Lennox, Elton John, Joss Stone, Robbie Williams, Scissor Sisters, Bob Geldof, UB40, U2, The Who, Sting and Pink Floyd contributed to the British contingent which started with U2 and Paul McCartney singing "Sgt Pepper's Lonely Hearts Club Band". Concerts also took place in other cities across the world including Paris, Rome, Tokyo, Philadelphia, Moscow and Berlin.

The Band Aid project and its spin-offs seem unlikely to be laid to rest. It's identified as the music industry's charitable organisation, and will doubtless re-surface when its powerful fundraising arm is needed to help those who are less fortunate than others. At time of writing, the Band Aid Trust has raised in excess of £100 million.

(See also Christmas 1984 and Christmas 1989)

2005

THAT'S MY GOAL/ IF YOU'RE NOT THE ONE/ RIGHT HERE WAITING
SHAYNE WARD

Perfect timing or chart hype? The Christmas UK number one single belonged to the winner of the second series of ITV's X Factor talent show. Facing the judging trio of Simon Cowell, Sharon Osbourne and Louis Walsh, a studio and home audience every Saturday night, were contestants of varying degrees of musical genres, hoping to be crowned the victor of the show. The winner would receive a recording contract with Simon Cowell's Syco label, co-owned by Sony Music Entertainment, and the much-publicised £1 million. In actual fact, only £150,000 was won in cash; the remainder paid for recording and promotional costs. However, to most, being part of the peak viewing music show was prize enough.

Photogenic sales assistant and club singer, Shayne Ward, born on 16 October 1984 in Manchester, won the grand final which was broadcast on 17 December 2005, when he was up against Newcastle sibling rock duo Journey South, and London bin man-cum-balladeer Andy Abraham. All three had previously recorded a version of "That's My Goal", with the winner having their version pressed and released as a single. Prior to the X-Factor, Shayne was a member of Destiny, a musical trio, who performed locally. He was a also a losing contestant on Popstars: The Rivals.

The three contestants (who were all at one point favourites to win) sang for survival on that December evening. Despite strong competition from ex-stripper, Chico; sultry songstress Maria Lawson and boy band 4 Tune, Shayne Ward proved to be the public's favourite from day one of the contest, with his commercial voice and humbling personality, perhaps contributing to his success. When Journey South was first eliminated, the battle for votes began in earnest for Abraham and Ward. It was later revealed that if just under 5% of the votes had swung in the opposite direction, Andy Abraham would have won – becoming the first black winner of a UK television reality show. As it turned out, he was also signed to Sony, where he scored a UK number two album "The Impossible Dream" in 2006, until Journey South replaced him at the top!

But with his success, Ward soon discovered the dark side of celebrity, when tabloids revealed that several members of his family, including his father, had prison time for serious crimes, so the gauntlet of the 'kiss and tell' was passed on to him.

"That's My Goal", a strong gospel-tinged power ballad reminiscent of Westlife's sound, was custom composed for the winner to sing. Released on 21 December it sold an estimated 313,000 copies within 24 hours, on its way to 742,000 sales in the first week to become the fourth fastest selling UK single of all time. It won the Ivor Novello award in the Best Selling Single category, among others.

Shayne's self-named album, released in April 2006, sold approximately 200,000 copies in its first week, to hit the chart at the top. It later passed platinum sales. A version of Bryan Rice's song "No Promises" followed the chart topper to peak at number two. Also during 2006, Shayne was diagnosed with vocal chord nodules and flew to Los Angeles to be successfully treated. In the November, he published his autobiography "My Story", and toured the UK on a book signing stint. Early the next year he embarked upon a solo tour across the UK and Ireland. His second album "If That's OK With You" was preceded by the single "No U Hang Up" in September 2007: both number two hits in their respective charts. "Breathless" was next with a no 6 placing, while the album hit platinum status. He followed this by the "Breathless" UK tour during 2008, debuting at the 02 Arena in London.

Two years later, Shayne's connection with Simon Cowell came to an abrupt end,, following the release of the comeback "Obsession" album, as the entertainment mogul concentrated on the careers of Susan Boyle and Leona Lewis. Nonetheless, the album was a top twenty UK hit. In 2011, Shayne diversified to star in the West End musical Rock Of Ages and performed in ITV's high profile skating series Dancing On Ice: he was voted off in the fifth round.

Shayne Ward can in future years look back and congratulate himself because as a male winner of the contest, his high chart status lasted longer than others in his position and in 2015 he was amongst names announced to join the cast of long running ITV soap Coronation Street, playing the ill-fated Aiden Connor after leaving his soap role , his re-invented acting career has gathered serious pace, and as of writing, announced an intended return to music performing a country-inspired soft rock style.

2006

A MOMENT LIKE THIS/ SUMMERTIME/ SORRY SEEMS TO BE THE HARDEST WORD
LEONA LEWIS

Series three of the top rated X Factor television show produced its first female, non-white, winner - and the programme's second consecutive Christmas UK number one single. The song was custom written by Jorgen Elofsson and John Reid for the winner of the first American Idol television contest to perform.

The reality talent show was by now being taken extremely seriously by chart compilers, as well as the general record buyer. It was now official: X Factor was taking no prisoners!

Leona Louise Lewis was born in the north London borough of Islington on 3 April 1985, to a Welsh mother and to a Guyanese father. A striking exotic looking blonde with a powerful vocal to match, she was an alumi of the prestigious Sylvia Young Theatre School. Later she was a pupil of Italia Conti, and the BRIT School, where she worked on her song writing skills and learned to play several instruments.

Determined to make a career as a singer/songwriter, the young Leona took several jobs to pay for demo recordings at the small Spiral Music imprint. The sessions comprised her own compositions, some of which resurfaced on the 'Best Kept Secret' project, released in 2009 by UEG Music, when the singer had reached international stardom. Leona could do nothing to prevent its release. However, for the time being, with no success forthcoming, and being ignored by major record labels, she almost considered taking a sabbatical, until her then boyfriend encouraged her to enter series three of the X Factor.

Dressed casually in a jumper and jeans, Leona's audition piece was a version of Judy Garland's iconic "Over The Rainbow" which impressed the trio of judges, who voted her through to the actual competition, when she was mentored by Simon Cowell. As expected, television viewers and the media, had already selected their favourites to win. They included the long haired, alpha male rocker Ben Mills, who made it through to the semi-final; ex-teen soap actor Ray Quinn, and the innately talented, Leona Lewis. On the tense evening of

16 December 2006, it was revealed that the winner would release a version of Kelly Clarkson's US chart topper "A Moment Like This", but beforehand the last two contestants – Leona Lewis and Ray Quinn – performed their interpretations before the studio and home audience, then waited for the voting outcome. The public voted Leona the winner, whereupon her note-perfect "A Moment Like This" was released four days later. Instant sales were highly impressive as they topped 870,000 copies, while download figures stood at 50,000 within 30 minutes of sales. The song went on to dominate the UK top spot for four weeks. The UK had finally found its own Whitney Houston-styled artist, but the question was would Simon Cowell allow her to fall from a great height and into the bargain bin of obscurity?

The answer was a resounding 'NO!'. Just two months after the contest win, Leona Lewis was signed to a five album deal for North America by legendary music mogul Clive Davis (who had mentored (the late) Whitney Houston into stardom) to release her recordings on the J Records logo. As the ink dried on the contract, it was publicly announced that the deal was worth £5 million. This unique close working relationship, orchestrated between Simon Cowell and Clive Davis, meant that Leona Lewis would work with A-listed producers and composers for her debut album to be titled "Spirit". The album with song writing/production credits that read like a who's who of contemporary pop and R&B – like Dallas Austin, Ryan Tedder, Ne-Yo, and Akon, Stargate, stormed into the UK chart at the top. It became the fastest selling album of all time when released late in 2007, and went on to sell in excess of eight million copies. Shortly beforehand, her second single "Bleeding Love", taken from the debut album, was a chart topper for seven weeks. In total, the title dominated twelve other countries including the USA, where Lewis became the first British female soloist to top the Hot 100 since Kim Wilde in 1987.

Like her or not, Leona became the new Princess of Pop. She was nominated for three Grammy and four BRIT awards, and won two MOBO awards - Best Album: for "Spirit", Best Video for "Bleeding Love". She was also voted Top New Artist in the American Billboard magazine. Leona became in demand as the modern female artist of choice, as she veered from the power ballad, where her voice could span four octaves, to a slight tempo shift. Leona went on to release singles for charity, like the double A-sided "Better In Time"/"Footsteps In The Sand" for Sports Relief; performing with rock legends including Jimmy Page at the 2008 Summer Olympics, and continued breaking records as typified by her 2009 release "Run" which became the fastest selling downloaded single.

As her second album "Echo" was released to great reviews and even greater sales in late 2009, with "Happy" its first single which peaked at number two, followed by "I Got You" in February 2010, Leona was the victim of an opportunist assault by a mentally unstable man while she attended a book signing session for her recently published autobiography "Dreams". Reputedly, her assailant had been a rejected contestant on X Factor, and the assault led to her cancelling immediate future promotional plans.

With the unfortunate incident behind her, she recorded "I See You (Theme From Avatar)", taken from James Cameron's successfully innovative sci-fi film, which was later nominated in the Best Original Song category at the 67th Golden Globe Awards. Her first tour in 2010, titled 'Labyrinth' was themed around the film. She went on to participate on the charity Helping Haiti single, which was a cover version of REM's "Everybody Hurts". It topped the UK chart early in 2010.

Leona Lewis opted to be more up tempo for album number three – "Glassheart", when the primary single release "Collide", was more dance slanted than her previous work. It reached the top five during the autumn of 2011. "Glassheart" hit the album chart at no 3. This was followed by "Hurt: The EP" in the December. Also this year, Leona performed in the American version of the X-Factor, and guested on the closing night of the Doha Film Festival. In 2012, she was the ambassador for BBC Radio 1's Hackney Weekend; released her next single "Trouble" to peak at number seven, followed by "Lovebird" which flopped. After the announcement that her American label J was disbanded by Sony BMG, her American output was via RCA Records.

A vegetarian since twelve years old, Leona is a leading figure in the World Society For The Protection Of Animals; a patron of Brentwood's Hopefield Animal Sanctuary, and PETA's person of the year in 2008, among other honours. She rejected a reported £1 million from Mohamed Al Fayed to open Harrods' 2008 sale because the store was the only UK outlet selling clothes made from animal fur. She has also launched her own perfume, and spearheaded the fashion company LOA Clothing Ltd.

As of 2023, Leona Lewis has now earned her place as one of the long line of 'Pop Princesses', to date the most successful UK contestant and champ of the X Factor brand.

After the tenure of Cowell/X-Factor/Syco ended, she was briefly snapped up by Universal/Island Records for a new recording contract, but meanwhile she remains the most successful UK X Factor contestant!

UK CHRISTMAS NUMBER ONES 1952-2022

2007

WHEN YOU BELIEVE/ HOME/ FLY ME TO THE MOON
LEON JACKSON

Another reality show victor; another Christmas number one single - a little predictable now don't you think?

Firmly embedded in the broadcasting schedules for autumn/winter was series four of X Factor and this time Dannii Minogue was an extra judge, while Sharon Osbourne announced her intention to leave this when this series ended. Series three had had memorable contestants - sibling pop duo Same Difference, Welsh operatic artist Rhydian Roberts, but it was a teenage Scottish jazz fan who was to be crowned this series' winner.

Leon Jackson, born in Whitburn, West Lothian on 30 December 1988, was previously employed as a sales assistant at a GAP store. He also practised karate and worked his way up to earning his black belt, but his ambition was to become a successful singer/songwriter. He also planned to study architecture at Napier University, but abandoned that when his singing ambitions took a serious hold and he entered the 2007's X-Factor.

When Glasgow was chosen as one of the audition places, Leon Jackson went along, won his heats, and new judge Dannii Minogue was his mentor. As this series progressed, Jackson was likened to Gareth Gates, Harry Connick Jnr, and, his musical hero, Michael Buble, and considered a likely winner.

On the night of the 15 December 2007, Leon reached the live finals before an estimated 12 million audience, and – apart from his own performance, he duetted with his mentor. When he was announced the winner by the viewing public, the result was tainted with controversy. It was alleged that votes for the runner-up Rhydian Roberts were 'blocked' giving Leon a clear win that night. However, this was later dismissed.

Leon Jackson was the latest recipient of the £1 million recording contract with Simon Cowell's Syco logo, via Sony BMG. A male take on the Whitney Houston/ Mariah Carey duet "When You Believe", which he performed prior to his victory, was recorded and released to secure the Christmas top spot this year for three weeks. It was the fastest selling single of 2007, selling

300,000 copies in one day. Also, Leon was the first Scot to secure the top spot over the Festive season. He then joined the X-Factor live tour in January 2008. However, his day was made when he won the Sunday Mail newspaper's 'Young Scot' award, and was twice invited by Michael Buble, to perform in concert with him.

Ten months on, he issued his debut album "Right Now" which hit the chart at number four, to peak at a spot higher, while his belated follow-up single "Don't Call This Love" also hit number three.

Meanwhile, Leon Jackson hosted his own web-only series Leon's Life, broadcast exclusively on the social network site, Bebo. The series not only documented his X Factor victory, but his first six months as a professional singer. "Creative" was the second single lifted from the album but was a download purchase only. It faltered at no 44 in the chart, while the follow-up "Stargazing" flopped. Following the failure of these releases he was dropped by Simon Cowell from the Sony BMG roster. However, to shake off the tag of 'winner's curse', Leon Jackson drastically changed his music as well as his visual identity. He switched from his beloved jazz influences to that of a traditional singer/songwriter, ditching the smart suits and the clean shave, for casual denim, the obligatory facial growth - and relocated to Los Angeles to hone his craft.

In 2010, after being voted the second biggest reality television show flop, Leon successfully showcased his new acoustic sound and visual image in Putney, London, followed by sell out crowds at the ABC in Glasgow, and the 02 Academy, Birmingham. A year later, he was a guest at the BRIT Awards ceremony, taking time out from teaching himself to play the piano and guitar. He also headed south of the border to honour several performing commitments, including one at Northampton's annual 'Party In The Park' event. This in turn, regenerated interest in his work as a recording artist once more.

He soon relocated to the USA and plied his craft as a songwriter for hire.

So, perhaps, let's not be so quick in claiming the 'winner's curse' has struck yet again!

UK CHRISTMAS NUMBER ONES 1952-2022

2008

HALLELUJAH/ CANDY MAN/ WITHOUT YOU
ALEXANDRA BURKE

Black British female soloists were starting to be taken seriously as a musical force to be reckoned with in the 2000s. While America had, Beyonce, Alicia Keys, Kelis, Ciara leading the way, Britain had Beverley Knight, Estelle, Jamelia, and Alesha Dixon, flying the flag. So, perhaps, it was no surprise that the winner of the fifth series of X Factor was a young, black songstress. It was her second attempt to win the crown.

Born on 25 August 1988 in the London borough of Islington, Alexandra Burke had musical pedigree. Her mother, Melissa Bell recorded as a member of Soul II Soul, and had worked with respected soul music elitists like Jean Carne. Apparently, Alexandra Burke sang to both Jean Carne and Stevie Wonder, before appearing as a 12-year-old contestant on the television talent show Star For A Night in 2000. She was beaten by future fellow chart artist Joss Stone. Undefeated, the young Alexandra worked at her craft by singing at weekends, and touring with the 'Young Voices', which raises funds for children with leukemia. In 2005, at the age of seventeen, she auditioned for the second series of X-Factor, and made it to the final seven in the '16-24 Years Old' category, mentored by Louis Walsh, but failed to make the final selection because he felt she was too young.

Three years later, and at the age of twenty, she auditioned again for the show and this time was mentored by Cheryl Cole in the 'Girls' category. Along her new musical journey, Alexandra attracted celebrity supporters including X Factor guests like Mariah Carey and Beyonce, as well as the rap artist 50 Cent. As the weekly live shows progressed, she was swiftly identified as the favourite to win, despite strong competition from the likes of Diana Vickers, Eoghan Quigg and that series runners up , the boy band, JLS.

Prior to her victory, Alexandra joined fellow finalists in the charity single release, a cover version of Mariah Carey's "Hero" which topped the chart for a trio of weeks in November 2008. Money raised from the single's sales benefitted Help The Heroes and The Royal British Legion. Alistair Darling, then Chancellor of the Exchequer, waived the VAT on all records sold because he supported the efforts being made by the X-Factor team. Again, like previous show winners, Alexandra sang the track that was to be her chart debut in the final – a cover version of Leonard Cohen's "Hallelujah". With votes totalling 58% in her favour, she beat JLS to the winning position. She was also the show's second female winner and an outright mentoring victory for the new judge Cheryl Cole. With the prize of a recording deal worth £1 million with Sony BMG – of which £150,000 was the cash prize for her - it took only a year for Epic Records to sign her to a £3.5 million recording deal for North America. Perhaps the company sensed that Alexandra had the potential of Leona Lewis, winner of the third X Factor.

"Hallelujah", a song Alexandra didn't particularly like, dominated the Christmas 2008 singles chart, with Jeff Buckley's version chasing her, and Leonard Cohen's original peaking in the top forty. The single not only launched Alexandra's career, but also renewed interest in both Leonard Cohen's life and work, and that of the late Jeff Buckley. Interestingly, as all three versions were set to chart, internet campaigns by Jeff Buckley fans gathered pace to prevent Alexandra Burke reaching the pole position, by urging 'followers' to purchase either of the other two versions. The story has an ironic twist because all three versions were released via Sony BMG labels, so whoever came out on top was irrelevant to the record company. They couldn't lose! It was reported that 576,000 physical copies and 105,000 downloads were shifted to secure the top spot for Alexandra, and to take the prize of the best selling single of 2008. The single also won the 2009 BRIT award for Best British Single, while she won the Best UK Newcomer category at the MOBO awards ceremony.

With Epic now on board taking care of the American side of her career, plans were afoot to record her first studio album, using the same tactics afforded to Leona Lewis, by engaging the cream of contemporary pop and R&B music, like Taio Cruz, Ne-Yo and StarGate. "Overcome" entered the UK album chart at the summit and was critically applauded by the sceptics. Prior to the album's release, the promotional single "The Silence" was issued to give fans a taster of what was to come. Further spin-off singles from the project included the belated follow-up "Bad Boys", featuring Flo Rida, which reached the top, passing platinum sales. It also won the BRIT award for Best Selling British Single. The bouncy "Broken Heels" followed, a top ten entry, and the percolating chart-topper "All Night Long", featuring Pitbull. Another BRIT award winner.

In 2009 Alexandra became the new face of Italian fashion designers, Dolce & Gabbana, and performed on The Royal Variety Show. A year later, she planned to team up with JLS to design their own fashion clothing under the company name of 2KX (2010). A year later their Underwear Collection went on sale. Alexandra then successfully undertook her first headline tour in 2011 under the moniker of the "All Night Long Tour", and collaborated with Swizz Beatz on the track 'Show Off' from the "Haute Living" album. Having deputised for an ill Kelly Rowland for two shows of the 2011 X-Factor, impressing the critics along the way, it was announced that Sony BMG's RCA imprint would handle Alexandra's UK releases from the second album onwards.

Alexandra Burke is well known for her charity work. In 2010, following the Haiti earthquake, she was the lead voice on a version of REM's "Everybody Hurts". Proceeds from its sales went to the Disasters Emergency Committee and The Sun newspaper's Helping Haiti Fund. Once again, VAT was waived by UK's prime minister, Gordon Brown, while REM forwent all royalties. Alexandra later visited Haiti as part of the Save The Children campaign. Later on, following her participation in the Peru Inca Trail Hike for Breast Cancer with other television celebrities, Alexandra helped spearhead the Save The Children's "No Child Born To Die" campaign in 2011. A year later she performed at the London launching of Shooting Stars, at the invitation of the charity's organiser, actor Samuel L Jackson, and then guested at charity functions to benefit the Great Ormond Street Hospital, and Breast Cancer Care.

Her second album "Heartbreak On Hold", with an electro house, R&B slant, had a similar dance/pop feel to her debut, and soon sparked comparisons with Leona Lewis who, for her third album, likewise embraced a dance orientated sound. When "Heartbreak On Hold" hit the shops and with internet downlands taken into account, the album peaked at number eight in the 2012 album chart, but any feelings of a career setback were eliminated when the pacey "Elephant" was extracted as a single to reach number three. A second track "Let It Go" followed.

Alexandra Burke's presence as a chart mainstay, though firmly established, was questioned when the radio stations that had offered that support so readily stopped not doing so. There was no surprise either that as interest in her music seemed to be lukewarm, she parted company with Simon Cowell and with Sony. However Burke made her American performing debut at the prestigious Apollo Theatre as part of a 'Apollo Theater Legends Hall of Fame 2013' line-up to celebrate the induction of legendary soul diva Chaka Khan, Burke's 'stagemates' were Patti Labelle, Jennifer Holliday and Mary J Blige.

Fresh from the Apollo gig Alexandra Burke reportedly signed with ex-Def Jam and Warner Bros executive Kevin Liles to guide her career, and released an EP, #NewRules.

In the meantime, she found herself hired as a replacement for the female lead in the West End revival of the film The Bodyguard, replacing British soul diva Beverley Knight and starring alongside Anglo-Australian actor Tristian Gemill, and impressed critics and theatregoers alike that she found herself contracted to The Bodyguard musical into 2016

Personally having settled into domestic life, professionally speaking, Alexandra Burke's presence as a chart mainstay and a public figure has now been firmly established.

UK CHRISTMAS NUMBER ONES 1952-2022

2009

KILLING IN THE NAME
RAGE AGAINST THE MACHINE

The power of the Internet should never ever be underestimated, because with help from a social networking site, Christmas 2009 had a unpredicted number one single. It was a sixteen-year-old track from an American group that courted controversy during its original nine year incarnation. It also denied the winner of the sixth series of X Factor its expected Christmas chart topper.

Rage Against The Machine (RATM) were formed in California in 1991, when guitarist Tom Morello left his previous unit, Lock Up, to start another band. Morello spotted rapper/vocalist Zach de la Rocha in a nightclub, and was so impressed that he approached him to be in his new, but as yet, unnamed rock group. With Zach de la Rocha on board as the front man, Tom Morello hired ex-Lock Up auditionee Brad Wilk as drummer and, as suggested by Zach de la Rocha, bass player Tim Commerford completed the line up.

The name Rage Against The Machine paid homage to a song Zach de la Rocha wrote for his previous unit Inside Out, and a phrase used by fanzine writer Kent McCloud. Heavily political and musically confrontational, Rage Against The Machine built up a commercial buzz while touring around California, and later issuing a self-titled twelve tracked demo cassette, which prototyped their forthcoming official debut album.

Record company interest was strong, including an offer from the Madonna-owned Maverick imprint, but the fiery quartet decided to sign with Sony's Epic logo, which apparently agreed to 'everything they asked for'. With the major label behind them, plans were set in motion to release their "Rage Against The Machine" album in a polished form suitable for the mainstream market. Released late in 1992, the album - which housed the 1993 hits "Killing In The Name", "Bombtrack" and "Bullet In The Head" - featured the controversial Malcolm Browne lensed image of a burning Vietnamese Buddhist monk called Thich Quang Duc protesting against the Vietnam war. The album went on to pass platinum sales.

During 1996, the group's second charting album "Evil Empire" peaked at number four, while the singles "Bulls On Parade" and "People Of The Sun" hit number eight and number 26 respectively. Three years on, "Guerrilla Road" faltered in the UK top forty, but later won a Grammy Award in The

Best Hard Rock Performance category. Their third album "The Battle Of Los Angeles" peaked at number 23 in the chart. Into 2000, "Renegades" stalled in the album chart at number 71, leaving the struggling "Sleep Now In The Fire" to reach the top fifty.

Let's fast forward to 2009, and the reason why, after a long absence and their initial break-up, they surprisingly grabbed the UK Christmas pole position. British husband and wife Jon and Tracy Morter started an internet campaign via the Facebook site, to protest against the Christmas chart domination by the winners of X Factor. They wanted to give another 'unrelated' artist a chance, so chose Rage Against The Machine's "Killing In The Name", which in 1993 had been a top thirty entrant. As a proportion of the profits from X Factor singles is always earmarked for a particular charity, so The Morters encouraged their followers to likewise donate to a charity. To this end, a splinter JustGiving page was formed to raise finances for the homeless charity, Shelter.

To the horror of both Simon Cowell and that year's contest winner Joe McElderry (who went on to top the chart in the New Year with "The Climb"), the power of the internet social networking gave life to the long defunct, but recently reformed, eclectic rockers to dominate Christmas sales. However, to the delight of Sony BMG who, of course, have the release rights to X Factor winners' releases, and to the recording rights to Rage Against The Machine's back catalogue, the record company dominated the top two places in the Christmas singles chart for the second year running.

If only for a short revival, Rage Against The Machine found themselves the latest musical 'blast from the past' getting the revived interest treatment, thus leading to their recorded work being made available once again. They had not mellowed with age either. During, a session for BBC 5 Live, the programme was riddled with their expletives, leaving the hosts Nicky Campbell and Shelagh Fogarty with no choice but to apologise profusely to the listeners.

The intense internet campaign behind the re-issue of "Killing In The Name", and the subsequent interest of Rage Against The Machine, was soon a memory. As for Joe McElderry, another reality show rescued his career, and another recording contract came calling. Ah well, the cultural buzz surrounding it all was great while it lasted, and as they say: that's showbiz!

2010

WHEN WE COLLIDE/ JUST THE WAY YOU ARE/ FIRST TIME EVER I SAW YOUR FACE/ NIGHTS IN WHITE SATIN
MATT CARDLE

Following the failure to top the singles chart last Christmas due to an intense internet campaign, the X Factor series, now in its seventh season, was determined that nothing this year would wreck the Christmas chart-topping dream of the selected winner. However, before that happened, the programme had to play down adverse publicity, because this series was by far one of the most controversial to date. Zimbabwean refugee Gamu Nhengu was threatened with possible deportation after a visa probe, Katie Waisel, whose kiss and tell escapades and colourful family background kept newspapers in print, Brazillian Wagner who clashed with judge Cheryl Cole in one show, and, last but not least, the alleged race row which saw promising black contestants dropped in favour of supposed mediocre white ones.

Aside from the controversy there was outstanding talent, like this season's runner up Rebecca Ferguson, Mary Byrne, and the last bandstanding One Direction. But the ultimate champ was a Hampshire-born struggling musician/singer, who was seen by many as a society 'underdog', latterly earning his stripes performing in various indie units.

Matt Cardle, born in the coastal town of Southampton on 15 April 1983. He was two years old when he was diagnosed with kidney cancer which resulted in having one removed. From the age of eleven he began playing guitar and composing songs. He then went to summer band camps as a teenager, before attending Stoke College, Suffolk, later studying a music course in Colchester.

In 2005 Matt Cardle joined the acoustic rock outfit Darwyn. They were awarded an Arts Council grant, released their album "When You Wake", and became a popular touring band. Four years on, Matt became a member of the rock outfit Seven Summers, and a year later their self-named album was released, distributed via the internet, to reach the top thirty on the Official

UK Album Downloads chart. During 2010, embarking upon a solo career, Matt auditioned for the X Factor performing an acoustic version of Amy Winehouse's "You Know I'm No Good", which secured his successful run throughout the series, under the guidance of his mentor Dannii Minogue.

As the weeks progressed, his acoustic/soft rock inspired material previously popularised by diverse artists like Roberta Flack, Britney Spears, Beyonce, The Moody Blues and Billy Joel, struck the right chord with the viewing public. It seemed they had taken this working class survivor into their hearts. The negativity that had surrounded this particular season was soon a distant memory as the public and the press singled out Matt Cardle as the possible favourite to win this series, and as it reached its conclusion, where he duetted with Rihanna, the public voted him the winner.

As usual, all the contestants, including Matt, released the annual X Factor charity single which this year was a cover version of David Bowie's "Heroes". And, as expected, it topped the chart. Meanwhile, Matt Cardle inherited the £1 million contract and the chance of recording the Christmas chart topper.

Previous winners have straddled the safe commercial options of pop or soul music, but Matt's category veered heavily towards the Radiohead/Coldplay market with a re-titled cover version of Biffy Clyro's "Many Of Horror". He had already previewed this as his winner's song on the show's final, but when released, the title was changed to "When We Collide" to dominate the singles chart for three weeks, passing the one million sales mark six months later; the fourth million-seller by an X-Factor winner. This had the knock on effect of re-igniting interest in the original version by Biffy Clyro, which charted in the top ten.

Rightly so, Matt Cardle was considered a show victor of promise; Britain's very own latter day working class music hero. His visual image may have belonged to an earlier era (protest folk singer imagery of guitar and cap), but his sound, when developed and established, was a saleable contemporary take on past influences. Simon Cowell took note of the potential audience that Matt would target, and handed over control of his latest charge to one of Sony's leading labels, Columbia Records, known for the rich back catalogue of the rock music's elite, like Bob Dylan, The Byrds, The Clash and Bruce Springsteen. He was the first ever X Factor winner not to be handled by Simon's Syco Music.

Almost a year on from his win, Matt's solo album "Letters" entered the album chart at number two with sales taking it into platinum status. A belated follow-up single written by Gary Barlow, titled "Run For Your Life" reached the UK number six, while a third, "Starlight", in December 2011 gained unlikely support with the clubland crowd, as numerous dance remixes secured its nightclub audience, taking it into the top ten of several dance charts. His fourth single (and third to be extracted from "Letters") was "Amazing", an extended play release, which he supported by the sold out "Letters" tour.

In 2012 Matt severed his ties with Columbia Records to sign with So What Recordings, the 'pop' division of the Silva Screen Music Group. The released his second album "The Fire", a top ten UK hit. Its offshoot single "It's Only

Love" was premiered and made available only via Matt's You Tube channel. Subsequently, it fared dismally by comparison to his previous releases. This was probably due to the fact that its availability was confined to an audio only medium. "Anyone Else", the second extracted single was issued in December 2012, the same month that he announced on his website his forthcoming "Unplugged Tour". Tickets for some of the dates were sold out immediately.

Cardle was on the move again this time releasing music through independent channels, with future material to be handled by Absolute Marketing (Universal Records for Europe) including his third studio album Porcelain, and in August 2013 a single to proceed the album, a duet with Melanie C titled 'Loving You' charted in the Top 20 In July 2013, The album embraced a more pronounced R&B/gospel flavour than his previous work.

Over a year later it was announced that Matt Cardle was cast in the role of Huey Calhoun in "Memphis The Musical" his first acting role whilst also announcing plans to record another album. At this juncture it is not wise to write off an artist like Cardle, as several recording artists even the most established suffer career setbacks as well as enjoying the high's of what a chart career can achieve.

If the right material is on offer for release and promotion, The charts, sales and (off course) Matt Cardle will all continue to be on familliar terms, providing that the media and the record buying public provide that vital network of publicity and support.

Matt Cardle is still proving there is a successful life after X Factor .

2011

WHEREVER YOU ARE/ NOW SLEEPS THE CRIMSON PETAL/ A SPOTLESS ROSE
MILITARY WIVES CHOIR

This Christmas chart topper evolved from that ever popular medium of reality shows, but not the one that had been playing Christmas dominator for four consecutive years. Rather a total opposite concept in which an unassuming hero forms a choir group from wives and partners of British military personnel.

Gareth Malone was the unassuming hero and the face of the cult BBC TV reality show "The Choir" who had, by the time, four successful series under this banner. And it was the fourth which struck an emotional chord with television viewers.

In April 2010 the first choir rehearsed in Catterick Garrison, following an idea mooted by two Scots Guards' wives whose husbands were deployed in Afghanistan. They advertised for women who were interested in joining a choir, giving them a focus while their husbands/partners were away fighting. A local music teacher came on board to formulate the idea, and the first choir was born. They contacted Gareth Malone to be auditioned for his television series. He agreed and the Military Wives Choir was born, featuring wives and girlfriends from two West Country military bases: the Chivenor Barracks in Devon, and the Royal Citadel, in Portsmouth. He worked with them locally, engaging them at functions like the Royal Military Academy's Passing Out dinner at Sandhurst, and Plymouth's Armed Forces Day.

In November 2011, the Choir performed "Wherever You Are", before HM The Queen, at The Royal British Legion's Festival of Remembrance, held at London's Royal Albert Hall. It was the perfect ending to the fourth television series. It was a natural progression that the song should be issued as a single. "Wherever You Are", created by Paul Mealor using extracts from correspondence between the members of the Choir and their partners, was released on 19 December 2011. With the realities of war striking a chord with the viewing public, radio soon added weight, and with the staunch support of BBC Radio 2 DJ Chris Evans, a campaign was soon under way to ensure this emotional single topped the Christmas chart.

Released on Universal's Decca imprint, initial sales were over 550,000, a figure guaranteed to elevate it to number one. Some of the money raised was donated to the Royal British Legion and the SSAFA Forces Help charities. Reports suggested that with heavy airplay "Wherever You Are" easily outsold the latest X Factor champs Little Mix. As Simon Cowell admitted defeat, Gareth Malone and the Military Wives enjoyed the song's success with humility and grace. Incidentally, this was the first time since Tom Jones' "Green Green Grass Of Home" in 1966, that the Decca label had issued a Christmas number one single.

The success of this project led to five other military choirs joining them to record the "In My Dreams" album, released under the name Military Wives. It topped the album chart during March 2012 within one week of sales, with £1 from each sale earmarked for the Military Wives Choir Foundation, which supported choirs being formed across the UK.

The Choir performed a new song "Sing", penned by Andrew Lloyd Webber and Gary Barlow, at the opening of the London Olympic Stadium. Written to honour HM The Queen's Diamond Jubilee, it was performed by representatives of the Commonwealth, with the Military Wives representing the UK. Producer, Jon Cohen helmed a second album titled "Stronger Together" which was painstakingly created using 24 different Military Wives choirs based across the UK, including the original five choirs from Portsmouth, Plymouth, Chivenor, Catterick and Lympstone. In total 700 women were featured on the album released late 2012, and to sustain the momentum, the same 24 choirs sent their alumni to London to record the album's title track promotional video. In October 2012 the Military Wives Choir coveted the Classical BRITS single of the year, and two months later they completed their year by appearing on BBCTV's Sunday evening programme "Songs Of Praise" and singing "In The Bleak Mid Winter" on The Queen's Speech transmitted across the Commonwealth on Christmas Day.

The concept and spirit of the Military Wives continues to grow, now numbering 67 choirs, all determined to entertain the public while highlighting the plight and courage of serving military personnel abroad.

UK CHRISTMAS NUMBER ONES 1952-2022

2012

HE AIN'T HEAVY HE'S MY BROTHER
THE JUSTICE COLLECTIVE

For the second year running the Christmas number one was not recorded by the winner of The X Factor but rather a cover version of a Bobby Russell and Bobby Scott composition first recorded by Kelly Gordon during 1969, later by The Hollies and Neil Diamond. Nonetheless, James Arthur, who won the television contest with "Impossible", a charity single with proceeds earmarked for Together For Short Lives.

This 60th Christmas UK number one single featured media personalities and musicians recording under the title The Justice Collective. The membership included Gerry Marsden, Robbie Williams, Melanie C, Beverley Knight, Holly Johnson, LIPA Gospel Choir, Kenny Dalglish, The Hollies' Bobby Elliott and Tony Hicks, Rebecca Ferguson, Paloma Faith and Paul McCartney, among others. This was the eighth Christmas single to feature McCartney. In similar fashion to the previous Band Aid charity singles, "He Ain't Heavy He's My Brother" was recorded to raise awareness and funds for the Hillsborough Justice Campaign. In April 1989 at Sheffield's Hillsborough Stadium during the FA Cup semi-final match between Nottingham Forest and Liverpool, a massive human crush resulted in 766 injured and 96 people lost their lives. Four years earlier, another footballing tragedy took 56 lives and injured 265 people. This time it was during a football match at the Valley Parade Stadium, Bradford, when the main stand caught fire. These were the worst stadium disasters in UK history and remain foremost in the minds of sporting fans and public alike.

Members of two groups, The Farm and The Clash joined forces to perform at an anti Sun newspaper concert following the phone hacking scandal at News International during 2011. After this, they formed The Justice Tonight Band as a touring band to raise awareness of the Hillsborough disaster across Europe. It was then decided to re-issue The Liverpool Collective's 2009 single "The Fields Of Anfield Road" but later that was side stepped for "He Ain't Heavy He's My Brother".

Released on 17 December The Justice Collective's version sold over 269,000 copies and raised money to help with the legal costs accumulated by families affected by the tragedy. All they wanted was justice!

UK CHRISTMAS NUMBER ONES 1952-2022

2013

SKYSCRAPER/ THE POWER OF LOVE
SAM BAILEY

The popular X Factor music contest, now in its 10th year, yet again struck gold with a Christmas chart topper after a three year hiatus. Ex-prison officer at HM Prison Gartree, Sam Bailey was announced winner, with a Syco recording contract worth £1 million and a guaranteed support spot on the UK leg of Beyonce's "The Mrs Carter Show World Tour" in 2014.

Born on 29 June 1977 in Bexley, London, and influenced by soul music and power ballads, Sam Bailey's musical ambitions began as a teenager when, with her friend Julie Nunney, she formed a Ska/Reggae duo named Girls Next Door under the aegis of Right Said Fred's musician Clyde Ward. Reputedly, Simon Cowell heard their single "Too Late" but considered the duo unsuitable for television. When Sam won "X Factor" the single was suddenly released online!

Having failed to break into the music business as one half of a duo, Sam performed at festivals and nightclubs, and on cruise ships. She initially auditioned for the X Factor six years earlier but failed to pass through the producers' round, so settled into family life and a regular job at HM Prison Gartree where she was nicknamed 'screwbo' because she reminded her colleagues, and later the tv viewing audiences, of Susan Boyle, runner up of Britain's Got Talent in 2009.

In 2013 Sam Bailey auditioned again for X Factor singing her version of Beyonce's "Listen" for which she received a standing ovation from the judges, led by Gary Barlow. Working her way through the categories, Sam was placed in the "over 25s" category to be mentored by Sharon Osbourne. She eventually won her way through to the final on 15 December 2013, had had the odds stacked against her being a 36-year-old pitting her voice against two young male singers – Nicholas McDonald and Luke Friend - both of whom were extremely marketable. During the final programme, Sam duetted with Nicole Scherzinger on "And I'm Telling You" from the musical/film "Dreamgirls", a version of Jennifer Rush's "The Power Of Love" and "Skyscraper". Sam Bailey won with votes topping one million from the viewing audience.

"Skyscraper", first recorded by Demi Lovato in 2011, was available for digital download immediately after the win was declared, and on 16 December her debut single was released to shoot to the UK pole position, passing silver status with sales of over 150,000. This was followed by her debut album "The Power Of Love" in March 2014 which entered the chart at number one, earning Sam the distinction of being the first X Factor winner to hit the top spot since Alexandra Burke in 2009 with "Overcome". Sam's album sold nearly 73,000 copies in its first week of release, the fastest moving album of the year. The planned UK tour with Beyonce was reduced to one date in Birmingham on 24 February because it clashed with the "X Factor Live Tour".

Also in March, Sam Bailey, married to Craig Pearson, with two children, announced she was ten weeks pregnant with her third child. On 10 September 2014, Bailey gave birth to a daughter Miley Beau. Three months prior she reputedly signed a deal to write her autobiography to be published at the end of 2014. It was announced in early 2015, that she and Syco had split,

In 2020, Sam joined a celebrity supergroup of called The Celebs, to raise money for worthwhile charities and released a cover of "Merry Christmas Everyone" on the Saga label. The song peaked at number two on the iTunes chart in time for Christmas.

In 2021 as a result of the Christmas charity single , Bailey was signed to a new record deal with Saga, and soon released a cover of Alannah Myles's 1990 hit "Black Velvet". The almost note perfect cover made the top three on the iTunes Rock Chart.

The future certainly seems bright for the latest 'girl next door' in whatever professional offers that may land on her mat.

2014

SOMETHING I NEED/ JEALOUS GUY/ HIGHWAY TO HELL/ MAN IN THE MIRROR
BEN HAENOW

The X Factor strikes again! – Series 11 of the popular Saturday night series proved to be captivating weekly viewing due to two popular contestants that never made it to the bottom two of the live performances and seemingly altered to be 'favourites' to win this particular series on a weekly (if not daily) basis.

The eventual winner, Ben Haenow (born 6 January 1985 in Surrey) an aspiring rock singer that grew up in humble beginnings alongside elder brother Alex, when they suffered personal misfortunes when their parents separated when they were at a young age leading to their mother to undertake three jobs just to survive, whilst a teenager Ben battled depression and alcoholism Having overcome such plight and by now in his early 20s, Ben was a founder member of a rock outfit named Lost Audio with Alex but by the time he made the decision to take the brave plunge to audition for the forthcoming X Factor series as a solo act, took gainful employment as a van driver to make ends meet.

Performing an emotive version of the known Bill Withers composition 'Ain't No Sunshine' before the four judges to a four-way yes, leading him to progress into the arena stage of the audition process, this time he successfully performed a version of The Rolling Stones classic 'Wild Horses' leading him to bootcamp and selected to be in the 'Over 25s' category (alongside runner up Fleur East, Jay James and 'wildcard' selection Stevi Ritchie) which this time was mentored by Simon Cowell.

For the next ten weeks as numerous contestants were gathering degrees of attention the focus equally was squared on Ben and also the eventual runner-up Fleur as both acts never fell foul of being placed into the bottom two of public votes and both finding themselves placed and predicted alternately as favourites to win this series.

On the night of the final live show, Ben Haenow found himself duetting with hit solo folk act Ed Sheeran on 'Thinking Out Loud' and performing a take on Michael Jackson's 'Man In The Mirror' track.

On the evening of 14th December 2014, it was announced that whoever the victor of the night would be, the final three were allocated their chosen tracks. The third place contestant Andrea Faustini was given a Whitney Houston track ' I Didn't Know My Own Strength' whilst both Fleur East and Ben Haenow were given 'Something I Need' a track previously recorded by the American rock-funk band One Republic.

As the evening progressed with Faustini eliminated, it was down to the two (from day one) public favourites with Haenow being announced as the winner with his version of 'Something I Need' being available instantly via download and then physical backed with his versions of John Lennon's 'Jealous Guy', ACDC's 'Highway To Hell' and (of course) 'Man In The Mirror' – all taken directly from his X Factor live performances.

'Something I Need' became the fastest selling single after Band Aid 30 and their latest update of 'Do They Know It's Christmas', when sales were estimated at 214,000 copies – making it the eventual Christmas number one single for 2014

Impressed by the sales and demands alone, Simon Cowell offered Ben Haenow a game changing birthday surprise. On 6 January 2015, the day of his 30th birthday, it was confirmed officially that Ben Haenow was a signed artist to Syco Records and then relocated to the US to start recording his self-titled debut album and soon released a belated follow up single taken from the it – a duet with one time American Idol winner Kelly Clarkson which entered the UK top 30.

2015

A BRIDGE OVER YOU
THE LEWISHAM & GREENWICH NHS CHOIR

The Christmas UK number one single for 2015 came from a rather unexpected source but borne (yet again) out of the reality TV show medium – but driving home the true charitable meaning and spirit of Christmas. Having previously appeared on the first series of Gareth Malone's BBC show The Choir: Sing While You Work, the concept behind the show was a competition between numerous workplace choirs, in 2012. The The Lewisham and Greenwich NHS Choir, who consisted of staff from across the NHS working spectrum, had ended the show as runners up. "A Bridge over You" was recorded in 2013, following the choir's appearance in the competition .

Various associated alumni saw the potential for a Christmas number one given the positive publicity that the show drew, so with the power of a social networking, a campaign to get the choir to top the UK singles for the Christmas period was launched two months prior to build momemtum.

The charity single "A Bridge over You" , is a clever medley-mashup of "Bridge Over Troubled Water" by Simon & Garfunkel and Coldplay's single "Fix You"

It was recorded at London's Angel Studios, arranged by Adam Morris with additional arrangement by the choir's conductor and musical arrangement, Peter Mitchell and released independently on behalf of the NHS Trust and released independently by the Lewisham and Greenwich NHS Choir and EmuBands – other musicians on the recording session included Liam Dunachie, Dan Ludford-Thomas, Christian Rae, Sam Weston and Ed Cusick

An accompanying promo video featuring numerous clips of working NHS staff was instantly made available for online viewing.

On the week of the Christmas charts, Canadian singer Justin Bieber, was the favourite for the Christmas week number one single with his "Love Yourself" single but having seen the praise and support for the Lewisham and Greenwich NHS Choir and the single, voiced his own endorsement for the song and choir and requested his followers to buy the single which in the process denied his own track from topping the Christmas chart. The online support worked as "A Bridge over You" eventually sold more than 127,000 copies

Plus the momemtum was raised with very public support from actor Stephen Fry, Labour Party leader Jeremy Corbyn and Radio 1 DJ Greg James (who in a heartfelt confession revealed an emotional debt to the hospital itself) amongst others.

The single raised lots of money for health charitable organisations with sales proceeds being split between numerous healthcare charities including Mind and Carers UK.

On the back of positive publicity Decca Records stepped in to offer the choir a recording contract and soon after released their debut album 'Something Inside So Strong', to tie in with celebrations to mark the 70th anniversary of the creation of the NHS.

UK CHRISTMAS NUMBER ONES 1952-2022

2016

ROCKABYE
CLEAN BANDIT
FT SEAN PAUL &
ANNE-MARIE

"It's something we never imagined would happen with "Rockabye" when we were writing and recording it. Thanks to everyone who has made this happen!"

It is fair to state that in recent times , the battle for the Christmas UK number one singles have been either from reality shows or for the good of charity But in 2016 it seemed that a return to a 'traditional' singles act claiming that festive chart topper and that unlikely source came from a classically trained/ influenced British quartet who all met as undergraduates at Jesus College located at the University of Cambridge in 2008 and whose band name derives from a Russian language depiction of the term "utter rascal"

The initial line up of Clean Bandit consisted of Grace Chatto (strings, cellist, percussionist, vocals), Jack Patterson (bassist, keys and saxophonist), Luke Patterson (percussion and drums) and Neil Amin-Smith who was the violinist and pianist. Amin-Smith left two months prior to achieving that much coveted spot.

Let's rewind back to their chart beginnings. This eclectic group whose influences run the gauntlet of not only classical but dance music too were signed initially to the independent Black Butter label but moved to the major Atlantic Records, released their first single "A+E" at the tail end of 2012 which failed to make any serious chart impression, but then after the release of their debut album "New Eyes" all facets of media started to sit up and take notice as their second single release "Mozart's Eyes" reached the top 20, and despite the faltering chart position of that follow up "Dust Clears" which peaked in the UK top fifty with gusto they bounced back with fourth single Rather Be – which featured guest vocals from current chart artist Jess Glynne which hit the UK top spot in early 2014 and ultimately it was the fastest-selling single , the year's second best-selling single in the UK and also won an American music Grammy award for Best Dance Recording in 2015.

Hot on the heels of the successful collaboration , the two performing entities joined forces for the release of "Real Love" which made number two.

They unsurprisingly soon found themselves in demand. Their presence was indeed felt on numerous showcases such as "Later With Jools Holland" and performing with the BBC Philarmonic Orchestra at Media City in Manchester plus embracing the global pull of promotional work to cement their arrival as the latest chart artists on the block.

They graced the charts again in mid-2016 with the new single "Tears" which enlisted X Factor winner Louisa Johnson to help provide guest vocals and were rewarded with a UK top five hit. Violinist Neil Amin-Smith for unknown reasons had decided to leave the group as they were crafting new material for a follow up album – the remaining trio decided to soldier on without him.

The first release without the prescence of Amin-Smith, "Rockabye" featured the hit Jamaican recording artist Sean Paul and British actress/singer Anne-Marie – which indeed became the band's second number one single in the UK and was ultimately the Christmas UK number one single for 2016. The single itself was a real labour of love for the band as they longed to collaborate with both Sean Paul and Anne-Marie.

The story behind the song is a humbling tale. Songwriter Ina Wroldsen, composed (with Jack Patterson) the lyrics about her son with the focus being a lullaby sung by mother to son – essentially it's universal message about all the sacrifices, sorrow and pain that mothers go through for their children and is also seen as being an anthem tribute to single mothers. The heart warming tale must have struck a chord of warmth with record buyers as beyond its Christmas chart-topping status, as the trick was repeated in seven other countries including Australia, Germany and Switzerland. It also entered the US Hot 100 whilst it was topping numerous global charts. The song's storyboard style promotional video which also featured both Sean Paul and Anne-Marie, was directed by the band's own film production company, Cleanfilm, primarily formed by members Grace Chatto and Jack Patterson to make their own music videos as well as for third party artists.

"Rockabye", despite it's relatively late release and peak, is one of 2016's biggest hits due to the power of downloads and online streaming. It went on to become an international chart topper for the band in eleven further global territories, peaking inside the top five in Canada and charted across the border to hit the top ten in the US. This young trio released "Symphony", as a follow up three months later which featured Zara Larsson on guest vocals and was another UK chart topper.

They soon found themselves at the mercy of rival record companies wanting to hire the trio to work on material for their own signings and as a result reportedly was pencilled to work on material for British 'blue-eyed' soulster Sam Smith. One of the most innovative acts on the UK charts to emerge for some time , releasing diverse singles and collaborating with eclectic artists

To date Clean Bandit have sold over 30 million singles and 1.6 million albums worldwide – despite the departure of one of their key figures the future is bright for one of the most innovative and exiting artists to emerge from Britain for a long while and to take on the global market too.

*Clean Bandit quote as told to the Official Charts Company/Reuters

UK CHRISTMAS NUMBER ONES 1952-2022

2017

PERFECT/ VERSIONS
ED SHEERAN

"This is an actual dream come true and I'm very proud and happy," "a very merry Christmas, happy holidays and a happy new year" – Ed Sheeran The Christmas chart for 2017 if anything seemed a return to 'Christmases past'!

A slew of classic festive recordings found themselves returning back into the UK top 40 during the sales in time for the Christmas week including, Wham!'s "Last Christmas", Mariah Carey's "All I Want for Christmas Is You", Pogues' "Fairytale of New York", the original Band Aid line-up with "Do They Know It's Christmas" whilst Brenda Lee's early festive favourite "Rockin' Around the Christmas Tree" were all battling for respectable chart space. Ultimately the 65th Christmas UK number one single went to an unassuming yet talented Yorkshire born singer/songwriter and musician who has steadily started to establish himself as a talented force to reckon with.

Singer/songwriter/guitarist and sometime actor Ed Sheeran (born Edward Christopher Sheeran on 17 February 1991) was born in the industrial West Yorkshire town of Halifax, but raised in the East Anglian county of Suffolk. As a teenaged undergraduate he attended the Guildford Academy of Contemporary Music in Surrey. In 2011, through independent channels he recorded and subsequently released an EP titled "No. 5 Collaborations Project" which subsequently lead to major label interest notably from the British branch of Atlantic Records. The legendary label assigned him instead to the revived Asylum subsidiary logo who issued his full debut album titled "Plus" / + was released during the Autumn of 2011 and was to be certified as platinum seven times over and by the following year he won the Brit Awards for Best British Male Solo Artist and British Breakthrough Act and an Ivor Novello Award for Best Song Musically and Lyrically (for the single "The A Team").

As his profile grew, both his demand and his recognition was increasing, he accepted an invitation to both work with the American country-turned-pop singer Taylor Swift on her fourth studio album project "Red" as well as acting as her support act for the North American leg of her Red Tour, whilst the "The A Team" single made its way over to America it found itself nominated for Song of the Year at the 2013 Grammy Awards and performing it with Elton John.

Sheeran's second studio album project , "Multiply"/ x was released during the Summer of 2014 and topped both US & UK Album charts as well as winning the 2015 Brit Award for Album of the Year, and received the Ivor Novello Award for Songwriter of the Year. Whilst the extracted single "Thinking Out Loud", he won two Grammy Awards at the 2016 ceremony: Song of the Year and Best Pop Solo Performance.

In early 2017 Sheeran's third studio album release , "Divide"/ ÷ was another global album chart-topper whilst two singles from the album, "Shape of You" and "Castle on the Hill" made him the first ever British soloist to have two singles enter inside the US top ten in the same week. Around the same time, he broke a UK chart record previously set by American crooner Frankie Laine (see Christmas 1953) 64 years earlier, occupying nine songs in the top ten of the UK Singles Chart

After the release of "Galway Girl", his next release was all set to take a complete life of it's very own after releasing a total of six versions (as well as numerous mixes) of the single "Perfect", including duets with modern day superstar R&B/pop queen Beyoncé and Italian operatic star Andrea Bocelli which including the numerous streams of sales patterns all in all resulted in achieving the 65th Christmas UK number one single – as of this writing total sales of "Perfect" was reportedly close to 85,000 including from aforementioned streams and downloads sales

"Perfect", saw a global release during the Autumn months of 2017 , eventually dominating a total of 18 countries including his core/base markets of the UK and the US, as well as the Australasian market throughout December 2017. It's demand resulted in "Perfect Duet", with Beyoncé was released alongside "Perfect Symphony" with Andrea Bocelli. "Perfect" inevitably became the UK Christmas number one single for 2017 due to sales pattern and sales visibility

The story behind "Perfect" is one of romantic inspiration and aspiration with a somewhat international flavour. Sheeran declaring on numerous occasions in relation to this particular track: "I needed to write the best love song of my career" and reportedly penned this melodic love ballad about his girlfriend who he knew from an earlier age but got together whilst meeting in the US, but also was inspired by meeting up with fellow singer/songwriter James Blunt whilst in Ibiza , both reportedly were listening to the music of hip-hop artist Future for songwriting inspiration.

The romantic and friendship themed, Jason Koenig directed promo video which was filmed at the Austrian ski resort of Hintertux co-starred Zoey Deutch with Sheeran and no doubt helped push sales within the video viewing generation.

As of this writing (2023) Ed Sheeran continues to make his presence felt with no signs of slowdown and is one of Britain's brightest hopes of fresh talent. An unassuming superstar, it is predicted he'll persist as a noted talent so long as his audience remains faithful, tapping into that craft of gaining new fans. Only time will tell.

2018

WE BUILT THIS CITY
LADBABY

The Christmas number one single for 2018 came from an unlikely source, the new media tool of 'internet superstar' - in this case a blogger of noted musicality from the East Midlands.

LadBaby - born Mark Hoyle in Nottingham, UK in 1987 - was the sudden discovery of this new medium of 'star seeking'.

With his YouTube channel, Hoyle adopted the alter-ego of 'LadBaby' whom alongside his wife Roxanne regularly blogged on his channel about the joys and trials of fatherhood, his musicality soon started to shine through with his 'fetish' for sausage rolls!

"We Built This City" previously a major hit for power ballad heroes Starship in 1985, was chosen with lyrical amendment alluding to sausage rolls as a recording debut and in December 2018 debuted at number one in time for the Christmas period of 2018, though billed as by 'LadBaby' it was a collaboration between husband and wife, making the Hoyles the first married couple to achieve a British Christmas number one single as well as the first official YouTube bloggers to top any chart. Perhaps unexpectedly It also charted on the US Billboard Rock Chart making the Top 50 and also in Australia on their digital chart making the top 40.

UK sales for this novelty remake went to the 'Trussell Trust' which benefited helping food banks.

The Hoyles were not done just yet...

UK CHRISTMAS NUMBER ONES 1952-2022

2019

I LOVE SAUSAGE ROLLS
LADBABY

In December 2019, a single "I Love Sausage Rolls", a comedic cover of The Arrows "I Love Rock 'n' Roll" which was popularised in the early 1980s by American rock diva Joan Jett was released with positive momentum.

Yet again a husband and wife team up. Released and promoted under the name of LadBaby, it secured the British number one spot for the Christmas period in 2019, this new version included new lyrics contributed by accomplished musician /songwriter Nick Southwood, this time on the US Rock Chart it managed to reach the top ten!

However the momentum was short lived as by the New Year the record slumped out of the top 40 completely and breaking records for the biggest drop from number one to 57. As with their previous Christmas number one single, sales proceeds went to The Trussell Trust.

Fast forward twelve months on...

2020

DON'T STOP ME EATIN
LADBABY

The Hoyles announced their new Christmas single, a comedic take on "Don't Stop Believing" renamed "Don't Stop Me Eatin", once more themed on Mark Hoyle's love of sausage rolls. An alternative version of "Don't Stop Me Eatin", which featured Roxanne Hoyle duetting with Ronan Keating.

Both versions combined in sales resulting in almost 160,000 copies securing it's charttopping domination for Christmas 2020 resulting at this juncture that LadBaby became one of the few singles chart acts in the UK to top the singles chart with their first three singles releases - yet again it's only American chart action was restricted to the rock-based radio stations who made it a top 30 hit on the nations Rock Chart.

The Hoyles at this time showed no signs of fading.

UK CHRISTMAS NUMBER ONES 1952-2022

2021

SAUSAGE ROLLS FOR EVERYONE
LADBABY

"We always said we'd only go for a fourth number one if we could make it bigger and raise even more money for the Trussell Trust. We approached Ed and Elton with an idea to do something that had never been done: to combine the music world with the social media world and join forces to make a difference to the people in the UK that need it most. Ed and Elton are pop royalty and they've both had huge success at Christmas, so we're honoured and excited to be coming together to help families this Christmas and bring back some true Christmas spirit with the power of sausage rolls!" - Mark and Roxanne Hoyle

This indeed came to fruition in December 2020 when the husband and wife blogging team LadBaby released "Sausage Rolls for Everyone" heavily adapted from the Ed Sheeran and Elton John musical team up track "Merry Christmas" and featured prominent guest appearances from both Sheeran and John. Like previous releases, it was released on the Frtyfve label and the sales proceeds yet again going towards the charity organisation Trussell Trust.

An alternative acoustic version of "Sausage Rolls for Everyone" was also released version with Sheeran and John replaced by The Food Bank Choir , both versions contributed to the almost 140,000 sales.

By the end of the year, "Sausage Rolls For Everyone" dropped dramatically from number one to number 29 in the charts. Across the Atlantic the comedic title managed a top five placing on the US Billboard Digital Sales chart, it topped the Billboard Holiday Sales chart and across the provinces in Canada it alsomade the top five on their digital sales chart.

Their fourth attempt to clinch the UK Christmas number one was very successful, by not just healthy sales margins alone but achieveing a UK chart record first: scoring four consecutive Christmas number ones – a feat which has not been seen in 70 years of the compilation of the Official Christmas UK Singles Chart.

2022

FOOD AID
LADBABY

As soon as December 2022 dawned, media eyes yet once again focussed on LadBaby. They announced, as expected, a planned release in time for the Christmas market, revealing that Sir Bob Geldolf, James 'Midge' Ure and the Band Aid Trust charity had given him permission to rewrite the lyrics to "Do They Know It's Christmas?" and release it under the LadBaby and to be retitled as "Food Aid".

The single was released a week before Christmas 2022 to help secure timely sales and interest. As well as featuring Hoyle's wife Roxanne, it also featured financial guru Martin Lewis. Monies raised from singles sales as agreed would be split between The Trussell Trust and the Band Aid Trust.

As the single dominated the Christmas number one spot LadBaby became the first act ever to achieve five consecutive UK Christmas number one singles.

Got a book in you?

Victor PUBLISHING

This book is published by Victor Publishing. Victor Publishing specialises in getting new and independent writers' work published worldwide in both paperback and Kindle format. We also look to re-publish titles that were previously published but have now gone out of circulation or off-sale. If you have a manuscript for a book (or have previously published a now off-sale title) of any genre (fiction, non-fiction, autobiographical, biographical or even reference or photographic/illustrative) and would like more information on how you can get your work published and on sale in print and digitally,
please visit us at:
www.victorpublishing.co.uk
or get in touch at: enquiries@victorpublishing.co.uk

Printed in Great Britain
by Amazon